FIGHTERS OF THE WORLD

JEREMY FLACK

Photography credits

Aermacchi: 9, 10t
Aero: 11
AIDC: 12, 13
Bob Archer: 89b
Bell: 17
BAe: 18b, 22, 23b, 81
Chris Brooks: 94
Grzegorz Czwartosz: 73, 88
DASA: 74
Dassault: 29, 30, 31, 32, 33, 34t, 35, 36, 38, 79
Embraer: 10b
Jeremy Flack: cover, 1, 3, 4, 5, 7, 8, 14, 15, 16, 18t, 19, 20, 21, 23t, 25, 39, 40, 41b, 42b, 43, 44, 45b, 47b, 48, 51t, 52t, 54, 57, 58, 59, 62, 64b, 65, 66, 68, 69, 70, 71, 72, 75,

80, 83, 84, 85, 86, 87, 89t, 90, 91, 92, 93
General Dynamics: 45t
Grumman: 46, 47t
Hughes: 42t, 56b
IAI: 50
Lockheed: 51, 52b, 53
McDonnell-Douglas: 24, 56
Mitsubishi: 67
E. Moreau: 37
SAAB: 76, 77, 78
USAF: 41t
Lindsay Peacock: 26, 28
Peter Steineman: 6, 27, 34b, 49, 55, 60, 61, 63, 64t, 82

ISBN 1 85648 263 4

Designed by Anthony Cohen
Printed and bound in China

INTRODUCTION

The evolution of the fighter aircraft has surpassed the dreams of the designers of the revolutionary fighting flying machines that were first encountered during the First World War.

These early aircraft were extremely flimsy and unreliable in terms of power and control. At the outbreak of the First World War, aircraft were still in their infancy. During the preceding century hydrogen-filled balloons were the only craft to take to the air with a military purpose. Soldiers used the balloons to reconnoitre enemy positions and for artillery spotting.

The advent of the aeroplane was seen by military planners purely as an advance in the balloon technology. Thus, the early military aeroplane was used for reconnaissance and for correcting the fall of artillery gunfire. Free from the restraints of the cable which had anchored their predecessors, the balloons, these aeroplanes were able to fly around the battlefield making a close inspection of enemy positions, then provide the details to the battlefield commanders.

The pilots who flew these early aircraft were probably not much safer than the soldiers who had previously manned the balloons, as they were still very vulnerable to ground fire. However, aeroplanes had the advantage of being a moving target, and, with the exception of the pilot and the engine, they were far more robust than the balloons. The pilots normally carried a pistol with them for self protection, in case they had to crash-land behind enemy lines.

At this time encounters between opposing aircraft were quite rare, and they were chivalrous occasions with pilots waving to each other. As aeroplane design developed, a second crew member was often accommodated to free the pilot from some of his tasks. This observer would often take a rifle with him to fire back at soldiers on the ground. The rifle could also be used to fend off potentially aggressive enemy aircraft. The crew of a Voisin of the French Aviation Militaire was reputedly the first to shoot down an enemy aircraft on 5 October 1914.

As aeroplane design developed during the First World War, both

SOPWITH PUP
The Sopwith Pup represented what was probably the first successful fighter, in that it performed well for its time, it was highly manoeuvrable and it was equipped with a machine-gun which was fitted with an interrupter. Unlike many of the aircraft of the period, the Sopwith Pup was a delight to fly and easy to control

SUPERMARINE SPITFIRE AND MESSERSCHMITT BF.109

The Supermarine Spitfire and Messerschmitt Bf.109 were adversaries throughout most of World War Two. The Spitfire first took to the air on 5 March 1936, while the Bf.109 had flown the previous September. The early Bf.109s suffered from poor performance, which was evident during operations with the Condor Squadron during the Spanish Civil War. The experience gained in Spain resulted in improvements in the power of this aircraft, which made it a tough opponent for the Spitfire when the two aircraft met over Europe. When Spitfire production was completed, a total of 20,351 aircraft of various versions had been built.

sides decided that a solution had to be found to combat the threat posed by enemy observation aircraft. As a result, various modifications were undertaken, which included the fitting of machine guns. The principal difficulty was where to place the guns on an aircraft and how the pilot operated them. The problems of propeller obstruction, gun reliability and reloading all had to be overcome. Initially deflector plates were fitted to the propeller, but the Germans developed an interrupter that enabled the machine gun to be synchronised with the propeller.

From this point on the fighter played an increasingly important role in modern warfare. However, during the 1920s, aircraft development was slow. The Schneider Trophy races probably made the greatest impact on the quest for speed. In 1931 the Supermarine S.6B won the race at a speed of 340.08 mph, although the front line fighters of that time were only capable of around 200 mph.

R.J. Mitchell used the experience that he had gained in designing the Supermarine S.6B and its predecessors to design the Spitfire. This aircraft was to enter service with the RAF in 1938 and remained in production throughout the Second World War with numerous developments being incorporated. The Spitfire and the Hurricane gradually replaced the obsolete but still operational biplane fighters of the RAF.

The fighter played a vital role during the Battle of Britain, when the Luftwaffe was tasked with eliminating the RAF as a preliminary to the planned German invasion of the UK. Commencing with an operational force of some 1,250 bombers and 1,000 fighters, large numbers of German bombers flew over London and other vital locations, escorted at least part of the way by the German fighters for protection. With an operational force of some 600–700 planes, the RAF launched formations of fighters to try to destroy the attacking German aircraft.

The Battle of Britain commenced on 10 July 1944 and finished on 31 October 1944. With up to 1,000 bombers attacking during any one day, the RAF fighters were stretched to the limit. By the end of the battle 1,733 Luftwaffe aircraft had been destroyed, but, most important, Hitler's plans to invade the UK were abandoned, thus changing the direction of the war completely.

The attacks by Royal Navy aircraft at Taranto and by the Japanese Navy at Pearl Harbour provided concrete evidence of how fighter aircraft could successfully attack and destroy major fighting ships. Aircraft were now able to attack targets with minimal warning and deliver substantial quantities of bombs and/or torpedoes quite accurately. In addition, long range Focke-Wulf Condor aircraft were supplying the German U-boats with target information on the convoys of ships that were crossing the Atlantic with vital supplies.

To combat these attacks, large numbers of a variety of fighters were built and flown by both sides to protect potential targets. In Britain only a few excelled in their role as fighters. The British Spitfire and Hurricane were being built in prolific quantities, as were the P-39 Airacobra, P-40 Warhawk/Kittyhawk, P-41 Mustang and F4F Wildcat in the USA. In Germany the Messerschmitt Bf.109 and Focke-Wulf Fw.190 were in production, while Japan was building the A6M Zero.

A successful fighter requires speed, manoeuvrability and firepower. During the early days of World War Two the speed of fighter aircraft was about 300 mph and this had increased to about 475 mph at the conclusion of the war. The speed that could be squeezed out of the piston engine was reaching a peak and other forms of power were being investigated.

The jet engine was showing promise. The Germans had designed

GLOSTER METEOR AND NORTH AMERICAN F-86 SABRE

The Gloster Meteor was the only Allied jet fighter to serve operationally during World War Two. This particular example is the later longer-nosed night-fighter variant – the Meteor NF.11.

The USAF F-86 Sabre entered service in 1949 and displayed a superior performance to other Western jet fighters of that period. The Sabre was 'blooded' in Korea, when it met up with the Russian-built MiG-15s. This aircraft had made its maiden flight just three months before the Sabre. Although the early examples were marginally inferior to the MiG, the quality of the American pilots gave them the edge.

The Sabre was widely used by the RAF and the Canadian, German, Japanese and Italian Air Forces, as well as those from Argentina, Bolivia, Ethiopia, Indonesia, Malaysia, Peru, Philippines, Portugal, South Korea, Tunisia, Uruguay and Yugoslavia.

TUPOLEV TU-95 'BEAR'

The Tupolev Tu-95 'Bear' was originally designed in the early '50s and was descended from the American B-29. As with the early B-52 Stratofortress of the USAF, these large bombers were fitted with tail guns to combat attacking fighter aircraft. With missile technology making the close encounters less likely, modern bombers are fitted with electronic jamming pods and flares to distract the missiles.

SHENYANG F-6 (MIKOYAN MiG-19), DASSAULT MIRAGE 5 AND GENERAL DYNAMICS F-16 FIGHTING FALCON

Up until ten years ago most countries sourced their military hardware either from Western sources or from the East. In recent years many countries are less likely to have a single source and they tend to shop around for the deals that suit them or the political climate that is compatible with their own.

This mixed formation of the Pakistan Air Force comprises the Shenyang F-6 (a Chinese built MiG-19), the French built Mirage 5 and the American General Dynamics F-16. Pakistan had relied on Western aircraft, but, following conflict with neighbouring India, replacements were not forthcoming, and 75 Shenyang F-6s were provided by China in the mid '60s. Later, orders were placed with Dassault for a number of Mirages of different variations. Despite the delivery of 40 F-16As and F-16Bs, the US Administration has placed an embargo on further supplies, due to Pakistan's continued progress with its nuclear programme. About $650 million had been already paid and demands have been made for this down-payment to be returned.

and built an axial-flow engine, which sucked air through a series of in line compressors before it entered the combustion chamber. The British design utilised a centrifugal-flow, which forced the air through two right-angles before entering the combustion chamber.

The Germans first flew their engine fitted in a Heinkel He.178 in 1939, while the British engine was fitted in the Gloster E28/39 and took to the air in 1941. The jet engine was originally conceived by an RAF cadet by the name of Frank Whittle in 1928, and it was thanks to his personal determination that the jet engine made progress in Britain. He took out a patent for the design in 1932 and became the first person in the world to run a jet engine on 12 April 1937.

Development of the jet engine progressed slowly towards power-ing an operational fighter. Fortunately for the Allies, Hitler decided that the Messerschmitt Me.262, which was capable of 540 mph, would be operated as a fighter-bomber, thereby reducing its performance. The Gloster Meteor was the first British jet fighter and initially it was used to combat the German V-1 flying bombs. As the Allies advanced through Europe, the Meteors followed operations, although aerial combat between the two jets did not take place. At the end of the war the Allies made much use of the German advanced technology designs, and development of the fighter progressed rapidly, with large numbers of aircraft being built, although many never progressed beyond prototype.

In 1950 the Korean War broke out and numerous combat aircraft were deployed. An early encounter with the MiG-15 provided a sur-

SUPERMARINE SPITFIRE AND PANAVIA TORNADO

The Supermarine Spitfire and the Panavia Tornado represent two RAF front line fighters some 50 years apart. When the Spitfire entered service, it was at the forefront of technology, replacing many of the old canvas and framework aircraft that had been designed in the '30s.

Today the Tornado fulfils much the same function – defending British airspace from any potential aggressor. However, the swing wing Tornado is capable of a performance far in excess of the much-loved Spitfire. Using its Foxhunter radar, the Tornado can detect hostile aircraft at a range of approximately 185 miles. Armed with four Sky Flash medium range air-to-air missiles and four Sidewinder short

range missiles, the Tornado is also fitted with a 27 mm Mauser cannon. The Tornado fighter has been designed to fly a Combat Air Patrol (CAP) several hundred miles outside national airspace lasting several hours. With the use of aerial refuelling that time span can be extended significantly.

The Spitfire and Tornado have featured in a number of airshows providing a synchronised display, with both aircraft flying similar manoeuvres showing the slow speed capabilities of the Tornado. The Tornado then turns on the power and flies a high performance individual display, including a demonstration of the variable wing sweep and power from the reheat.

---

prise for piston engine powered US pilots. The arrival of the F-86 Sabre narrowed the gap between the opposing airforces, although this was more as a result of pilot skills rather than of aircraft performance. However, the arrival of later Sabre models with improved performance turned the tables, and large numbers of North Korean MiGs were shot down.

From the early days until the early '50s the main armament of the fighter aircraft was the gun. This had evolved from the early machine guns through to the more powerful cannon which required the pilot to fly close to the enemy and point his aircraft at the opposing one. During World War Two air-to-ground rockets were

carried by some aircraft to attack ground targets. These led to the development of unguided missiles that could be fired in salvoes at the target aircraft. As technology improved, infra-red and radar guidance heads were fitted to the missiles.

The centrifugal-flow engines gave way to axial-flow designs, which brought substantial increases in power and fuel efficiency. By the mid '50s Lockheed had built the Mach 2 (1,400 mph) F-104 Starfighter.

Missile technology was also progressing, with the introduction of Semi-Active Radar Homing (SARH) missiles, which depend on the radar from the attacking aircraft to illuminate the target. Once

BOEING SENTRY AEW.1

Radar plays a major role in flying tactics today, to the extent that an aircraft can be tracked several hundred miles away if flying at a reasonable altitude. As radar travels in a straight line, modern military tactics include flying at low level to remain in the radar shadow provided by the hills and to maintain an element of surprise. To beat the low-flying aircraft, the radar stations were elevated by fitting them in an aircraft. This effectively reduces the shadow areas and extends the horizon.

The Airborne Early Warning (AEW) aircraft such as the USAF Boeing E-3 Sentry or Sentry AEW.1 (illustrated) is a transport aircraft with a radar dish mounted on top. Inside the crew monitors the radar returns and communicates with friendly forces, intercepting any hostile aircraft by means of secure communications links.

sensed, the missile's guidance system directs the missile until it hits the target, or the proximity fuse detonates as it passes close by. The Infra-Red (IR) missile detects the heat source and uses this to maintain contact and guide the missile home.

During the early air-to-air missile development, the SARH missile achieved greater accuracy than the IR. The IR could easily be diverted by the sun or reflections from water. It could only track aircraft from the rear, as this was the angle from which it could get a good 'fix' on the engine exhaust. The modern missiles have reversed this trend, as IR missiles are now capable of accurately tracking and hitting a target head-on. The other advantage of the IR missile is that it is passive, in that the launch aircraft provides no guidance signals, unlike the SARH, which immediately gives away the attacking aircraft position. The missiles can be designed for short range or long range. The US Navy Phoenix can destroy a target over 100 miles away.

The relative ease with which air-to-air missiles can be fitted to an airframe has resulted in the modification of aircraft from a wide range of functions to give them a fighter capability. Also, the cost of high-performance fighter aircraft is now so high that the pure fighter aircraft is becoming a rare breed. Instead, a number of multi-role aircraft include fighter as one of their roles. The air-to-air missile can also be fitted to attack or patrol aircraft that may be required to fly into hostile territory without fighter protection.

For the purposes of this book the definition of a fighter aircraft is an aircraft or helicopter that has the capability of shooting down another.

RADAR SCREEN

The radar returns are shown on a screen like this, which shows the radar picture from an RAF Sentry monitoring the Bosnian air exclusion zone. The purple lines indicate the national borders, while the dotted red line marks the exclusion zone. The dotted green line extending from inside the exclusion zone is the route that the UN relief aircraft take from Sarajevo to Zagreb and the green dots represent aircraft returns. The yellow markings along the green line are identified UN aircraft.

Should any unidentified aircraft appear inside the exclusion zone on the radar screen, fighters would be directed to investigate. There have been a number of such incursions in this conflict, especially by helicopters which are forced to land. On a couple of occasions aircraft have been shot down by fighters on UN patrol.

AERMACCHI MB.326

The design of the Italian Aermacchi MB.326 commenced in 1954, with the prototype taking to the air for the first time on 10 December 1957.

The MB.326 is a simple, yet strong two seat basic jet trainer. A batch of 15 pre-production aircraft was built initially, followed by total orders for 85 for the Italian Air Force. The first aircraft entered service with the Italian Air Force during February 1962.

A ground attack variant was offered with six underwing stores pylons, but the Italian Air Force foresaw no requirement for such an aircraft. Tunisia was the first country to place an order for eight of the MB-326B. This was followed by other orders from Ghana, Tunisia, Australia and South Africa, where it was known as the Impala. Australia and South Africa undertook local assembly or licence production. Even the airline Alitalia took delivery of four.

Initial deliveries were fitted with the 1,134 kg st. Rolls Royce Viper 11, while the MB.326GB was fitted with the more powerful 1,547 kg st. Viper 20, which resulted in a significant improvement in performance. Orders followed from Argentina, Zaire and Zambia. Brazil wanted 112 of the MB.326GC model, and arrangements were made for licence production by Embraer as the AT-26 Xavante.

A single seat operational trainer and light attack aircraft followed in the early '70s with 230 mm cannons in the nose and an increased number of six underwing hard points. Designated the MB.326K, it was capable of carrying a range of weaponry, including bombs, rockets, reconnaissance pods and air-to-air missiles.

Fitted with the Viper 623, the MB.326K was a reasonably powerful aircraft which could carry about 1,814 kg of weaponry. Orders were received from Dubai, Ghana, South Africa and Tunisia.

AERMACCHI MB.339

The MB.339 is a second generation jet trainer built by Aermacchi. Its structure is much the same as that of the MB.326 design, but with a revised forward fuselage and the Rolls Royce Viper 632 turbo-jet. Construction commenced following an initial Italian Air Force requirement. The first flight was made on 12 August 1976.

The MB.339 has a much improved rear cockpit view for the instructor. As with the MB.326, the MB.339 has been offered in the close support role in addition to the advanced trainer. Apart from the Italian Air Force, operators of the MB.339 include Ghana, Malaysia, New Zealand, Nigeria and Peru.

AERMACCHI/ALENIA/EMBRAER AMX

The AMX is a close interdiction, tactical air support and reconnaissance combat aircraft which has been developed jointly by Aermacchi and Aeritalia (now Alenia) of Italy and Embraer of Brazil. A total of seven prototypes were built - three by Aeritalia, two by Aermacchi and two by Embraer. The first made its maiden flight on 15 May 1984.

Although the basic airframe is the same, each country has fitted the AMX to meet their own requirements. The Italian built model (above) has a more sophisticated cockpit fit than the Brazilian, while the Italian has one 20 mm cannon compared to the Brazilian, which has a pair of 30 mm cannons. The Italian AF will be using the AIM-9

Sidewinders, but the Brazilian AF will be using its own MAA- 1 Piranha AAM (below).

A two seat trainer has also been developed, with the second seat taking the location of the forward fuel tank in the basic single seat design. Additional variants have been proposed for the roles of Electronic Warfare (EW) and maritime attack.

The Italian requirement is for 110 single seat and 26 two seat trainers, while the Brazilian is 65 including 14 trainers, although their total could rise to 150.

AERO L-39 ALBATROS

The Aero L-39 Albatros was selected as a trainer aircraft to replace the Aero L-29 Delfin for the Air Forces of the Warsaw Pact. Seven prototypes were constructed, of which two were for static tests. The first flew on 4 November 1968. A batch of ten pre-production aircraft entered production in 1971, followed by full production the following year.

The Albatros was initially used for elementary and advanced jet training as the L-39C. Several variants of the L-39 have since emerged. These include the L-39V, which is a single seat target tug, the L-39ZO improved training version with a reinforced wing and the L-39ZA for ground attack and reconnaissance. The latter is fitted with a twin bar-rel 23 mm gun located in an under fuselage gun pod, and also has four hard points on the reinforced wing. These can be used to carry a range

of weaponry, including bombs, rockets, drop tanks or air-to-air mis-siles. The final Albatros variant is the L-39ZA/MP, a multi-purpose model which is fitted with Western avionics, as well as a Head Up Display (HUD).

An upgraded Albatros variant is the L-59 with improved thrust from the DV-2 turbofan and modernised cockpit instrumentation. This has been ordered for the Air Forces of the Czech Republic, Egypt and Tunisia. A further development is the L-139 which is powered by the Garrett TF E731-4-1T in place of the original Ivchenko AI-25.

The L-39 looks likely to achieve as much success as its predecessor, the L-29, of which more than 3,500 were built. Currently production already exceeds 2,800 and they are operated in 16 countries world-wide.

AIDC CHING-KUO

The AIDC Ching-Kuo is the ambitious Taiwanese development of an indigenous fighter. This expensive project was the direct result of the USA's attempts to improve its relationship with China, leaving Taiwan relatively isolated from a diplomatic point of view, and unable to rely on the USA for its future defensive equipment as it had in the past. This project commenced in May 1982, following the US refusal to allow purchase of the Northrop F-20 Tigershark or General Dynamics F-16. Design proceeded with assistance from various US companies, and four prototypes were constructed. The first took to the air for the first time on 28 May 1989.

Work on a pre-production batch of 10 aircraft commenced in 1990 and the first production batch of 60 has been authorised. The Chinese Nationalist Air Force has a requirement for some 256 of the Ching-Kuo, which includes around 50 two seat trainers. They will be used to replace the F-5E Tiger IIs and the F-104 Starfighters.

The Ching-Kuo is armed with a 20 mm M61A Vulcan cannon. It has two hard points under the fuselage plus a further four under the wings. These can be used to carry the indigenous Sky Sword I and II air-to-air missiles, Hsiung Feng II anti-shipping missiles or bombs or rockets.

AIDC A-3 LUI-MENG (above)

The AIDC A-3 Lui-Meng is a single seat development of the AT-3. It is fitted with the Westinghouse AN/APG-66 radar and fire control system. It has a close air support, night attack and strike capability in addition to its training role. It can carry 2,721 kg of external stores.

AIDC AT-3B TZU-CHUNG

The AIDC AT-3B Tzu-Chung is a two seat, twin turbofan close-air support variant of the AT-3A trainer. An initial order was placed for 60 AT-3As, and production commenced in 1982. Two prototype AT-3Bs were converted from the AT-3A, and the first made its maiden flight in 1989. An order was placed for 20 AT-3As to be converted to AT-3Bs.

The AT-3B has a weapons bay beneath the rear cockpit into which a range of weapons can be fitted, including machine gun packs. The AT-3B can be fitted with a centreline and four under-wing pylons, as well as a pair of wingtip launch rails. It can carry a total of 2,721 kg of weapons, including bombs, rockets and air-to-air missiles.

ATLAS CSH-2 ROOIVALK

The Atlas CSH-2 Rooivalk is a South African designed attack helicopter. Its main role is anti-armour, for which it can be fitted with eight or sixteen anti-tank missiles. It has been designed for deep penetration with a 700 km range, although this can be increased to 1,260 km with external fuel tanks. Its close-air support capability is provided by a chin mounted 20 mm cannon plus up to 88 68 mm rockets. In addition to the cannon, for heliborne support the Rooivalk is fitted with up to four V-3 Kukri air-to-air missiles, with which it is capable of shooting down attacking enemy aircraft or helicopters. The Rooivalk can also be used in a reconnaissance role.

As well as being a quiet craft, the Rooivalk has a low radar and Infra-Red (IR) signature to reduce the chances of it being detected. It is fitted with various threat detection, warning and jamming electronics, as well as redundancy and damage tolerance for critical systems.

In 1994 the Rooivalk was submitted for the British Army attack helicopter in competition with the Eurocopter Tiger, Bell AH-1 Cobra Venom and AH-64 Apache. While this would have been inconceivable only a couple of years ago, the recent political changes in South Africa have made it possible for South African companies to compete on the international market.

AVIOANE IAR.99 SOIM

The Romanian Avioane IAR.99 was designed as an advanced trainer/light ground attack aircraft. The prototype made its maiden flight in December 1985, and deliveries are currently being made to the Romanian Air Force to replace the L-29 Delfin.

The IAR.99 is powered by a Rolls Royce Viper Mk.632-41 turbojet and has a maximum speed of 865 km/hr. It is fitted with two hard points under each wing, onto which bombs, rocket or gun pods, drop tanks or other stores, including air-to-air missiles, can be fitted. An under-fuselage attachment is available for a 23 mm gun pack. It has a 2 hour 40 minute endurance and a maximum range of 1,100 km.

MIG-21 **2000**

BEDEK MiG-21

The **Bedek MiG-21** upgrade is indicative of the contemporary emphasis on providing refurbishment options for tired airframes around the world. There are large numbers of older generation airframes, such as MiG-21s, F-5s, A-4 Skyhawks and Mirages, for which many countries cannot afford replacements, but which can be brought up-to-date with new avionics and airframe overhaul at a reasonable price.

Bedek of Israel is a company in the refurbishment market which has taken a MiG-21, stripped the airframe and rebuilt it to incorporate modern Western avionics. The customer then receives back a

virtually new aircraft, with much improved performance, due to the new avionics fit. As over 6,000 MiG-21s have been built, as well as the Chinese copies, there is a huge potential market for this type alone.

Other types that have been upgraded by Bedek are the Northrop F-5 and Grumman tracker.

India recently entered into a contract with Mikoyan to upgrade 125 of its MiG-21bis to include a derivative of the radar which is installed in the MiG-29 as well as adding some Western electronics.

BELL AH-1 HUEYCOBRA

The Bell AH-1 HueyCobra was a company development during the early '60s for an armed helicopter. Inital designs were based on the Bell 47, but this was dropped in favour of the UH-1 Iroquois. Around the same time the US Army decided that it needed an armed heli-copter in Vietnam. The prototype first flew on 5 September 1965.

The US Army was impressed and within days ordered two pre-pro-duction prototypes. The following April a production order was placed with Bell for 110. By 1971 well over 1,000 had been ordered.

When it was originally built, the AH-1 Cobra was a formidable machine, and its reputation as such has been sustained over the years by the addition of various upgrades. Fitted with a 20 mm or 30 mm gun or 40 mm grenade launcher in a chin turret, it has two stub wings on which a range of weapons can be fitted, including 7.62 mm Minigun pods, and seven or nineteen tube rocket pods. Later variants can be fitted with eight TOW anti-tank missiles while the latest AH-1W can be fitted with the Hellfire anti-tank missile, Stinger and the AIM-9 Sidewinder air to air missile.

A twin engined variant AH-1G was designed for a US Army

requirement, but resulted in an initial order from the US Marine Corps as a SeaCobra in 1968. A further increase in engine power from the GE T700 in place of the T400 introduced the A-1W SuperCobra.

On 24 January 1989 the first of a four-bladed AH-1(4B) Viper variant took to the air. Modified from an AH-1T, the Viper has an additional two weapon stations on the wing stubs and can operate the AGM-122 Sidearm air-to-ground missiles. Two of the rotor blades can be folded for easy stowage aboard ship. It is planned to modify existing AH-1Ws of the USMC with this rotor.

Another version of the Viper with advanced cockpit features has been designed and proposed by GEC for the British Army Air Corp's attack helicopter and named Cobra Venom.

The HueyCobras were deployed in considerable numbers during the Vietnam war and later variants were despatched to the Middle East and used effectively during Desert Storm.

In addition to the US Army and US Marine Corps, customers for the AH-1 include Iran, Israel, Jordan and Spain.

BRITISH AEROSPACE HAWK T.1

The British Aerospace Hawk was designed as an advanced flying and weapons training aircraft. The first aircraft flew on 21 August 1974.

The Hawk T.1 entered service with the Royal Air Force in November 1976 and gained an excellent safety record. From 1979 it has been operated by the Red Arrows and flown at numerous airshows throughout the world.

For weapon training the Hawk is fitted with one centre line hard point and two wing pylons. Normally these are used for a 30 mm Aden gun under the fuselage plus practice bomb pods under the wings.

An additional role of local air defence was allocated to the Hawk. To enable them to undertake this role, 89 aircraft were modified so that they could carry the Sidewinder missile, and these craft were designated Hawk T.1A. They were then tasked with flying local air defence while the Tornado would operate a considerable distance out.

BRITISH AEROSPACE HAWK 100

The Hawk 100 is a current export model which, in addition to the equipment fitted to the 60 Series, has a ring laser Inertial Navigation System (INS), Head Up Display/Weapons Arming Computer (HUD/WAC). It also has a colour multipurpose head down display, stores management display, Hands On Throttle And Stick (HOTAS) controls and radar warning receiver. The Laser ranging and Forward Looking Infra-Red (FLIR) are options which can be added.

BRITISH AEROSPACE HAWK 200

The Hawk has an excellent development potential which BAe continues to exploit. The single seat Hawk 200 was developed as a private venture as a lightweight multi-role combat aircraft from the successful two seat advanced trainer used by the RAF. The prototype first took to the air on 19 May 1986

The single seat Hawk 200 makes use of the space and weight saved from the second cockpit to stow additional role-dedicated equipment. It is fitted with the AN/APG-66H radar to provide navigation and target information in air-to-ground, maritime and air-to-air roles. Each variant is capable of carrying a range of air-to-air missiles as well as operating in the close-air support role.

The Hawk has had a successful export career, benefiting from the selection by the US Navy as the T-45A Goshawk. In this context the aircraft is used purely for aircrew training.

Apart from the RAF order which was for 175 aircraft, the Hawk is flown by the Air Forces of Finland, Indonesia, Kenya, Kuwait, Oman, Saudi Arabia, South Korea, Switzerland, UAE and Zimbabwe. It is also on order for the Royal Malaysian Air Force.

BRITISH AEROSPACE NIMROD

The Nimrod is a maritime patrol aircraft adapted from the Comet airliner and operated by the RAF. During the Falklands War these aircraft were required to patrol in the south Atlantic, some 4,000 miles from the nearest airfield – well beyond the range of any fighter. As a result, they were fitted with Sidewinder air-to-air missiles for self-defence.

BRITISH AEROSPACE HARRIER GR.7

The British Aerospace Harrier is the West's only operational Vertical/Short Take Off and Landing (V/STOL) combat aircraft. It was a development of the Hawker P.1127, which first flew on 21 October 1960 and the Kestrel, which took to the air for the first time on 7 March 1964. The first production Harrier made its maiden flight on 31 August 1966.

This revolutionary family of aircraft utilised an innovative engine design which introduced the term 'vectored thrust'. The principle of this engine was to divert some of the compressed air out of the side of the engine to exit through a pair of rotatable nozzles. Meanwhile, the rest of the air continues through the combustion chamber and exits through another pair of rotatable nozzles located further aft. The result is that, with the nozzles at right angles to the line of flight and pointing straight at the ground, sufficient lift can be generated to lift the aircraft vertically. By slowly rotating the nozzles, the thrust from the engine provides forward thrust and the lift will then be provided by the wings.

The Pegasus was the revolutionary vectored thrust engine which enabled this family of aircraft to take to the air. Initially the thrust to weight ratio meant that the P.1127 had limited capabilities, but as a prototype it proved that this complex theory could indeed be put into practice.

When the Harrier GR.1 entered service with the RAF in April 1969, it became the first operational V/STOL aircraft in the world. A total of 120 Harriers were purchased (including 6 development aircraft) for the RAF, which flew them in the close-air support role of ground

attack and reconnaissance. Capable of operating from near the front line from roads, matting laid in a field or from woods, the Harrier was able to operate in support of ground forces at very short notice and without major ground-based support.

It was in 1982, during the Falklands War, that the Harrier came into its own when fourteen RAF Harriers were flown down to the south Atlantic to join the Royal Navy Sea Harriers aboard the carriers HMS Hermes and HMS Invincible. With minimal practical training in ski ramp take-offs, the RAF pilots successfully operated their Harriers from the carriers in their close-air support role.

While the Americans were designing the AV-8B, BAe were designing a replacement for the RAF Harrier. Although it is a similar aircraft, the RAF Harrier GR.5 included a number of differences which were considered necessary for the RAF's close support role in the European arena. This includes a moving map display, as well as various avionic changes. The GR.5 also has the Rolls Royce Pegasus Mk.105, two additional hard points for Sidewinder missiles and a Radar Warning Receiver (RWR). The further addition of a Forward-Looking Infra-Red (FLIR) sensor for night attack capability has resulted in the GR.7 variant, and all previously built GR.5s will be modified to conform to this. The first GR.5 flew on 30 April 1985.

For training purposes thirteen two seat Harrier T.10s have been ordered. These are based on the USMC TAV-8B, but fitted with the FLIR, as fitted to the GR.7, thus retaining an operational capability in wartime, while normally being flown as a trainer.

BRITISH AEROSPACE SEA HARRIER FRS.1

In 1975 an order was given to BAe by the MoD to develop a variant of the Harrier GR.3 for the Royal Navy to operate from the new Through Deck Cruisers. The resulting Sea Harrier retains a 90% similarity in airframe, powerplant and mechanical systems. However, the nose and cockpit area is the main structural difference. Internally, the two aircraft are quite dissimilar due to the different roles which they undertake, with only a 10% commonality in avionics. The Sea Harrier first flew on 20 August 1978.

The Sea Harrier FRS.1 was designed to provide the Royal Navy Fleet with fighter cover as well as operating in the reconnaissance and strike roles. It was fitted with the Ferranti Blue Fox radar for air-to-air and air-to-surface roles, and could be fitted with the Sea Eagle anti-shipping missile as well as Sidewinder missiles.

While the first of the new Through Deck Cruisers were being built, a RN officer, Lt. Cdr. Taylor, claimed that the Sea Harrier's take-off performance could be enhanced significantly by using a ramp. Following trials, it was discovered that the Sea Harrier could carry an extra 1,500 lb of fuel or weapons when a 'ramp assisted' take-off was used. As a result, HMS Hermes and all three 'Invincible' class ships, as they came to be known, were modified to include a 'ski ramp'.

In 1982, 28 Sea Harriers out of the total fleet of 32 at that time were deployed to the south Atlantic. They were to operate from the Royal Navy carriers HMS Invincible and HMS Hermes during the Falklands War, during which they flew some 2,000 operational sorties and destroyed 22 Argentinian aircraft.

The Indian Navy has purchased three batches of single seat Sea Harrier Mk.51 and Mk.60 trainers to operate from their two carriers – INS Vikrant and INS Viraat, which was previously HMS Hermes.

SIDEWINDER

The AIM-9 Sidewinder is a fire and forget Infra-Red (IR) homing missile developed for short range engagements. It was developed in the early '50s by the US Naval Weapons Centre at China Lake, and first launched on 11 September 1953. It is a simple and cheap AAM missile which led to the construction of approximately 95,000 of the original AIM-9B in the USA and Europe.

Over the years the Sidewinder has increased in sophistication and many AIM-9Bs have been rebuilt. The missile guidance is based on an Infra-Red source seeker in the missile head. When it is activated and locked onto a source, the pilot receives an audible signal. At this point the missile is fired, detonated by the proximity fuse, and should destroy the enemy aircraft. Although this appears to be a simple procedure, the missile could be distracted by the sun or reflections on water, and its effectiveness diminishes in bad weather.

In 1977 a new, much improved generation of the Sidewinder entered production – the AIM-9L. This leap forward in the seeker design not only resolved the earlier problems, but also resulted in the missile being all aspect (i.e. the target aircraft can be at any angle and not limited to aiming just from the rear). Combined with an improved warhead, this development makes the AIM-9L a formidable missile. Development and production of further unproved variants continue.

SEA HARRIER FA.2

The Sea Harrier FRS.1 is currently undergoing a Mid-Life Update (MLU) to incorporate the latest avionics, including the replacement of the Blue Fox radar with the Ferranti Blue Vixen Pulse-Doppler multi-mode radar and the capability to operate new missiles. The resulting version with its distinctive larger radome is the Sea Harrier FRS.2, which first flew on 19 September 1988.

While retaining the ability to carry the AIM-9L/M Sidewinder AAMs, the Sea Harrier FRS.2 systems have been designed to operate the Advanced Medium Range Air-to-Air Missile (AMRAAM). At the same time the FRS.2 can still carry Sea Eagle anti-ship missiles, bombs or rockets and the 30 mm Aden Cannon.

In January 1994 an order was placed for a further eighteen new Sea Harrier FRS.2s. Subsequently all Sea Harriers have been re-designated FA.2.

EUROFIGHTER 2000

The Eurofighter 2000 is the product of a revised EFA in the light of the termination of the Cold War – a development which almost saw Germany withdraw from the project. This fighter eventually made its maiden flight on 27 March 1994. It had been preceded by the EAP (Experimental Aircraft Programme) which was a proof of concept aircraft that first took to the air on 8 August 1986.

A European Staff Requirement for Development of EFA was signed by the four nations' (UK, Germany, Italy and Spain) Chiefs of Air Staff in 1987. This specified a high performance, agile combat aircraft, optimised for the air superiority role with a comprehensive air-to-surface role. It was expected to exceed the capabilities of existing and future adversaries, and yet maintain a reduced cost of purchase and operating compared with competing aircraft.

The EFA has been designed as an unstable aircraft which utilises a highly advanced computer system to retain control, enabling faster response. Pilot control is fed through a quadruple 'fly by wire' system into the computer, which then outputs the appropriate signals to the various controls. Much use has been made of carbon-fibre materials and other advanced materials to reduce weight yet maintain strength and durability.

Due to its small size, EFA has a small radar cross section, which, together with the use of radar absorbent materials, provides the aircraft with a stealthy radar signature. The aircraft is also fitted with a number of passive sensors, such as the Infra Red Search and Track System (IRSTS), which will enable the pilot to launch his attack sequence without using his radar and thereby indicating his presence to an enemy.

To assist the pilot, EFA is fitted with the state of the art 'glass cockpit' containing three full colour multi-function displays on which all key tactical flight information is presented, plus a Head Up Display (HUD). Pilot control is through a Hands On Throttle And Stick (HOTAS) which replaces the conventional 'joystick'. The pilot also has a direct voice input system enabling him to operate some procedures by speech. The helmet also has a mounted symbology system which maximises head up flying for the pilot

The ECR 90 radar that is fitted to EFA is one of the most advanced systems for the long range detection and acquisition of multiple tar-

gets. It is highly ECM resistant and incorporates a threat analysis to identify and prioritise targets for the pilot. A Defensive Aids Sub-System provides the pilot with an all-round threat assessment and can make responses automatically or manually.

A total of thirteen hard points give EFA a high load capacity and ability to accept various missile configurations. External fuel tanks can be fitted to three hard points. For the air-to-air role a mixture of at least ten ASRAAMs and AMRAAMs can be accommodated, while seven hard points can be utilised for the ground support role. A multi-role configuration might include six air-to-surface missiles or bombs plus six air-to-air missiles plus external fuel tanks together with an internal gun.

Seven development aircraft have either been or are being built with the various companies responsible for certain major components. The front fuselage and foreplanes by BAe, MBB – centre fuselage and fin, Alenia and CASA – rear fuselage, Alenia – left wing, BAe and CASA right wing. The production workshare will be allocated according to the actual number of aircraft ordered by each nation, with each company having final assembly for that number of aircraft.

BAE/MCDONNELL-DOUGLAS AV-8B HARRIER II

The AV-8B Harrier was a development of the AV-8A, which was evolved from the BAe Harrier as used by the RAF. US interest in the British V/STOL programme dates back to the early days of the Kestrel, when a Tripartite squadron was formed with the British, US and German Air Forces. When this was disbanded, only the British retained a major interest and the Harrier subsequently entered service.

The success of the Harrier aroused the interest of the US Marine Corps, which eventually ordered 110 AV-8A Harriers. Subsequently twelve AV-8As were ordered on behalf of the Spanish Navy to operate from their carrier Principe de Asturias. The USMC, like the RAF, found their Harriers a very useful asset, to the extent that they commenced a programme for a replacement when the AV-8A was approaching the end of its life.

The only replacement was the AV-8B Harrier II. Although this designation implies that the AV-8B Harrier II was merely a modification of the original AV-8A, the Harrier II is a completely re-designed aircraft. The prototype AV-8B, which was in fact a heavily re-built AV-8A, first flew on 9 November 1979. The first new AV-8B did not take to the air until November 1981.

The AV-8B has a new supercritical wing with a greater span and area, as well as increased fuel capacity and large slotted flaps. The additional lift together with the additional power from the Pegasus 11/F402-RR-406A vectored thrust turbofan enables the Harrier II to operate at a much higher all-up weight. The cockpit is raised to provide the pilot with a bubble canopy and thus a better view, as well as providing additional space for avionics. The under-fuselage gun is fitted with devices to improve the ground cushion in VTOL flight while reducing the hot gas re-circulation.

During the Gulf War 86 AV-8B Harrier IIs were deployed to the region to operate either from carriers, Saudi bases or from forward operating bases just behind the front lines. During the conflict these Harriers flew over 3,300 missions, dropped nearly 6 million pounds of ordnance and maintained over 90% mission capable.

Two new versions of the AV-8B are now flying. The first to evolve was the Night Attack Harrier II with the more powerful Pegasus 11-61/F402-RR-408 engine. Like the RAF GR.7, it is fitted with Forward-Looking Infra-Red (FLIR) sensors. During night operations the pilot wears night vision goggles and the cockpit is fitted with compatible lighting, so that the aircraft is now capable of operating on all but the darkest of nights. The first Night Attack Harrier II first flew on 26 June 1987 and entered service during September 1989.

The latest version is the Harrier II Plus. In development with funding from the US, Italian and Spanish Governments since 1970, this aircraft first flew in September 1992. This Harrier variant is fitted with the Hughes AN/APG-65 multi-mode radar. In addition, it has ECM and enhanced avionics which provide the pilot with an improved situational awareness and navigation during poor weather and low visibility conditions. It also provides an improved air-to-ground capability in day, night and adverse weather, as well as improved air-to-air capability and survivability.

In addition to 27 new build aircraft, an order has been received for the first 4 of a scheduled 73 existing day attack AV-8Bs to be converted to this improved standard. Eventually all USMC AV-8Bs will be completed to this specification. The re-manufacture involved the fitting of a new fuselage with the APG-65 radar and night attack systems together with the more powerful Rolls Royce Pegasus F402-RR-408 engine. This will result in significant cost savings in comparison with the production of a completely new aircraft.

CASA C-101 AVIOJET/E-25 MIRLO

The Spanish **CASA C-101 Aviojet** was designed to meet a Spanish Air Force requirement for a basic and advanced jet trainer. A project presentation was made in 1974 and a contract subsequently awarded. The first C-101 took to the air on 27 June 1977. The C-101 Aviojet was subsequently given the military designation E-25.

As with most other recent jet trainers, the C-101 has been given the additional task of weapons training. From there, the next step has already been taken towards giving the aircraft a strike role. With only small changes the C-101/E-25 can be fitted with a range of weaponry including guns, rockets and air-to-air missiles on the six underwing pylons.

In addition to the Spanish Air Force, the C-101/E-25 is operated by the Air Forces of Chile, Honduras and Jordan.

DASSAULT MIRAGE III

The Dassault Mirage III was France's first Mach 2 fighter. It was designed as a high performance multi-role fighter with a low unit cost. This delta winged design was configured from a range of variants, so that, by using the same basic airframe and fitting it out to fulfil its specialist roles, the aircraft costs were reduced. The ruggedness of the airframe was also a major contribution to its popularity with a large number of foreign customers. The prototype took to the air on 17 November 1956 and the first of ten pre-production Mirage IIIAs flew on 12 May 1958.

The Mirage IIIC was the first production example. This was an all weather interceptor, and 95 were built for the French Air Force with others being flown by Israel, South Africa amd Switzerland. It was fitted with the CSF Cyrano I radar and armed with Matra 530 or Sidewinder AAMs. A total of 244 were built. The IIID was the trainer variant of the IIIO. 453 of the IIIE interceptor were built and fitted with the improved Cyrano II radar which gave an all weather capability and increased performance from the Atar 9-C turbojet. The IIIB was the two seat trainer of the IIIE, and was comparable in terms of performance. The IIIR was a further variant of the IIIE, but with a new nose housing reconnaissance cameras. The IIIO and IIIS were licence built examples by Australia and Switzerland respectively.

Other countries which have been operators of the Mirage III include Argentina, Brazil, Israel, Lebanon, South Africa, Spain, Venezuela and Pakistan (illustrated).

When production stopped, over 1,300 Mirage IIIs had been built in three different countries. Futher production was carried out in an unlicenced form in Israel as the Nesher and Dagger.

DASSAULT MIRAGE 50

The Dassault Mirage 50 is a variant of the Mirage 5 using some Mirage F.1, 2000 and 4000 technology and fitted with the more powerful Atar 9K-50. This resulted from the successful installation of the engine in the Mirage III for South Africa. It first flew on 15 April 1979.

Although the performance of the Mirage 50 was superior to the Mirage 3/5, it was not favoured with the same sales success as the rest of the family. The Chilean Air Force order for sixteen aircraft was the only order received.

Along with a number of the Mirage III/5/50s that remain in service with various air forces, the Chilean Air Force Mirage 50 is in the process of being updated with new avionics, as well as foreplanes to provide enhanced manoeuvrability. The Chileans have re-designated this updated aircraft the Pantera 50C.

DASSAULT MIRAGE 5

The Mirage 5 was developed from the Mirage III with reduced avionics and increased fuel and weapons to fulfil an Israeli requirement. The prototype first flew on 19 May 1967.

The Mirage 5 was adapted primarily for the ground attack role. It is armed with two 30 mm cannons and its seven hard points are capable of carrying a wide range of bombs, rockets, external fuel tanks or AAMs. In addition to the strike model, the Mirage 5D is the two seat trainer and the 5R is the reconnaissance variant.

An order for 50 Mirage 5Js was placed by Israel. Shortly after the first aircraft flew, Israel and Egypt were in conflict in what became known as the 'Six Day War'. An embargo on military equipment to Israel was imposed by France just prior to this war. Following lengthy

negotiations which resulted in the aircraft remaining in France, the money paid by Israel was refunded. Eventually the aircraft, which had all been built, were re-worked and entered service with the French Air Force.

The Mirage 5 achieved reasonable export success, with examples being sold to Columbia, Egypt, Gabon, Libya, Pakistan (illustrated), Peru, UAE, Venezuela and Zaire. In addition, in 1968 the Belgian Air Force selected the Mirage 5 as a replacement for its obsolete F-84s. A total of 106 aircraft were ordered, which comprised a mixture of 5BA single seat fighters, 5BD two seat trainers and 5BR single seat reconnaissance aircraft. They were all licence built by SABCA in Belgium.

DASSAULT MIRAGE 2000

The Dassault Mirage 2000 is the latest generation of the Mirage family and made its maiden flight on 10 March 1978.

The Mirage 2000 retains the delta wing design of the Mirage 3/5 which it is replacing. This is a Mach 2.2+ fighter with multi-role capabilities and it is powered by a SNECMA M53 turbofan. It is fully fly-by-wire controlled, with much use being made of composite materials to reduce weight.

The Mirage 2000 is armed with two 30 mm DEFA 554 guns. In addition, it has nine hard points enabling it to carry a wide range of loads of up to a total of 6,000 kg. Apart from fuel tanks, these loads can include the Super 530 and Magic AAMs (seen here being launched), bombs and rockets, various pods for guns, ECM and even buddy refuelling.

DASSAULT MIRAGE 2000C

This Mirage 2000C is armed with a pair of the Matra R.530 air-to-air missiles. In addition to 7 prototypes, the French Air Force originally ordered a total of 372 Mirage 2000 (C, N and Ds), although 54 were subsequently cancelled. Other customers include Abu Dhabi, Egypt, Greece, India and Peru.

DASSAULT MIRAGE 2000D (above)

The Mirage 2000D is a two seat, all weather strike aircraft derived from the 2000N, and first flew on 19 February 1991. It has been given a re-designed cockpit to form a better interface between the crew and the weapon system. It has a long range, high speed, very low altitude ability with an automatic terrain following capability.

A wide range of conventional weapons can be carried by the Mirage 2000D, including laser guided bombs, and rockets, and it can be fitted with the **ASMP** medium range air-to-ground nuclear missile. It is shown here fitted with two **LGB**s and an Atlas designator plus two R.550 Magic AAMs.

DASSAULT MIRAGE 2000C-RDI (below)

The Mirage 2000C-RDI is the 2000C that has been fitted with a Thomson-CSF/Dassault Electronique RDI radar in place of the RDM and the SNECMA M53-P2 engine replacing the M53-5.

This Mirage 2000C-RDI is fitted with a pair of Magic 2 close combat air-to-air missiles on the outer pylons and a pair of Matra Super R.530s on the inner pylons for long range.

DASSAULT MIRAGE 2000C-RDI

This Mirage 2000C-RDI is also fitted with the Magic 2 and Super R.530 air-to-air missiles. It is seen here during aerial refuelling from a Boeing KC-135FR Stratotanker.

Most fighters and strike aircraft are capable of receiving fuel from a tanker aircraft. This is known as a force multiplier, as it enables fewer aircraft to undertake the same task. Providing fuel to an aircraft while it is airborne enables it, in the case of a fighter, to remain on patrol for a longer period without the need to return to base to refuel.

DASSAULT MIRAGE 2000-5

The latest member of the family is the Mirage 2000-5, which is fitted with an advanced cockpit similar to the Rafale and new RDY radar capable of tracking eight targets simultaneously. The Matra Mica AAM is carried by the Mirage 2000-5 with the Matra Super 530D and BAe Sky Flash AAMs as alternatives. Although the Mirage 2000-5 has been optimised for air-to-air missions, for the air-to-ground role a range of laser guided bombs, rockets, missiles and the Apache stand off dispenser can be carried.

DASSAULT MIRAGE F.1CR

The Dassault Mirage F.1 is a swept wing variant of the Mirage family of fighter aircraft. The swept wing was substituted for the delta to reduce drag during manoeuvring and to shorten the take-off and landing distances. The Mirage F.1 was developed as a private venture and the first prototype took to the air on 23 December 1966.

The design of the Mirage F.1 allows a 45% greater fuel capacity which trebles the endurance of patrol or interception missions over the Mirage III. It also doubles the combat radius for the attack role. In addition, the Cyrano radar had been improved and the Matra R.550 Magic air-to-air missiles became available, making the Mirage F.1 highly capable.

The Mirage F.1 was designed for a variety of roles. The F.1A had a reduced avionics package with a higher fuel/weapons carrying capability similar to that of the Mirage 5. The Mirage F.1B is the two seat trainer, as is the F.1D, and the F.1C is the single seat all-weather interceptor. A sub-variant in the form of the Mirage F.1CR undertakes reconnaissance missions, while the F.1E is designed for the multi-role version.

This Mirage F.1CR is painted in a desert camouflage and was deployed to the Gulf War in 1992. It was photographed here in formation with a Jaguar while on operations over Iraq.

DASSAULT MIRAGE F.1JE

When production of the Mirage F.1 was completed in 1991, a total of 731 aircraft of all variants had been built. The French Air Force ordered 251 altogether, including 5 prototypes.

The Mirage F.1 has been exported to Ecuador (illustrated), Greece, Iraq, Jordan, Kuwait, Libya, Morocco, Qatar, South Africa and Spain. During the Iran/Iraq war, over 100 Exocet missiles were fired from the Mirage F.1, one of which hit the US frigate USS Stark.

DASSAULT RAFALE B

The Dassault Rafale is an all-weather multi-mission combat aircraft designed to meet the needs of the French Air Force and Navy into the next century. It is capable of air-to-ground/sea attack, air defence and superiority, nuclear strike and reconnaissance. The designs of the Rafale are more than 95% common in terms of systems and 80% common for structure and equipment. The Rafale A prototype first flew on 4 June 1986. The two seat Rafale B is for the French Air Force and first flew on 30 April 1993.

The Rafale design was for a highly agile aircraft. To achieve this objective, Dassault used the delta wing shape, and fitted the Rafale with controllable foreplanes. More than 50% of the structural mass of the airframe comprises new materials, especially carbon composite, to reduce weight but maintain strength. The aircraft is also fitted with two **SNECMA M88** turbofans.

For the nuclear strike role, when fitted with the weapon and external fuel tanks, the Rafale will have a greater radius of action than the existing Mirage IVP.

DASSAULT RAFALE C

The Rafale has fourteen hard points (thirteen for the naval version), including five wet points for fuel tanks. A wide range of weaponry can be carried, including up to eight of the new Mica air-to-air missile, AS30L air-to-surface missile, Apache stand-off weapon dispenser, ASMP medium range cruise missile and the supersonic ANS anti-ship missile. Up to eight tons of external stores can be fitted and the aircraft/stores interface enables a rapid and varied reconfiguration according to requirements. In addition the Rafale has an internally mounted 30 mm DEFA 791 cannon with a high rate of fire.

DASSAULT RAFALE M (above)

The Rafale M is the French Navy variant which first flew on
12 December 1991. During 1992 it spent nearly six weeks at the US
Naval Air Engineer Centre at Lakehurst and the US Naval Air Test
Centre at Patuxent for extensive equipment testing, especially the
landing gear during catapult take-offs and arrester landings. During
the catapult launch the Rafale is subjected to a 5g longitudinal acceleration. During the landing the aircraft can be descending towards the
deck at up to 1,200 ft per minute and it can then be subjected to a

4.5 g deceleration. In April and May 1993 the Rafale M took to sea
aboard the French Navy carrier Foch for further trials. The naval variant of the Rafale will require a substantially strengthened structure, as
well as salt water corrosion protection.

This formation (below) shows the three variants of the Rafale family.
Rafale B leads while Rafale C is nearest and Rafale M is on the far side.
The Rafale has been designed to replace the Crusader and Super
Etendard of the French Navy and the French Air Force Jaguars.

DASSAULT SUPER ETENDARD

The Dassault Etendard had been operated by the French Navy since the early '60s. By the end of that decade it was becoming obsolete. The SEPECAT Jaguar M was designed to be the replacement and a prototype was built. In 1972 this was cancelled and the A-7 Corsair or A-4 Skyhawk was proposed. In the end a much developed Etendard, named Super Etendard, was selected. Two prototypes were converted from existing Etendards and the first flew on 28 October 1974.

The Dassault Super Etendard was designed as a carrier-based fighter bomber. The general configuration is similar to that of the Etendard, but it has been almost completely re-designed and fitted with upgraded avionics. The first new Super Etendard flew on 24 November 1977. Originally there were plans to build 100 aircraft, but due to budgetary restrictions this was reduced to 71 to operate aboard the French Navy carriers Foch and Clemenceau.

The Super Etendard is fitted with two 30 mm guns and has five hard points onto which a range of weaponry or fuel tanks can be fitted . These can include tactical nuclear weapons, Exocet air-to-surface missiles and the Matra Magic AAMs.

A batch of fourteen was also ordered by the Argentinian Navy. Shortly after deliveries commenced, Argentina invaded the Falklands. Supplies had also commenced of the Exocet anti-shipping missile and these were used in attacks against the Royal Navy Task Force. As a result HMS Sheffield and the container ship Atlantic Conveyer were hit and destroyed.

In 1983 France also leased five Super Etendard to the Iraqi Air Force complete with Exocet missiles to provide an anti-shipping capability against Iran.

DASSAULT–BREGUET/DORNIER ALPHA JET

The Alpha Jet is the result of a Franco-German agreement to produce a light twin engine two seat basic and advanced training aircraft for the French and German Air Forces. The prototype made its first flight on 26 October 1973 and deliveries commenced in 1977.

The Alpha Jet is powered by a pair of Larzac 04 turbofans which give the aircraft a maximum speed of Mach 0.85 and an endurance of up to three hours at altitude. It is fitted with four under-wing hard points onto which a range of weapons can be fitted. This example is fitted with the Exocet air-to-surface missile plus a pair of Magic AAMs.

Following the German reunification, drastic cuts in defence spending have reduced the Luftwaffe requirement for the Alpha Jet and most of the fleet was retired. In the summer of 1993 an agreement was reached between the German and Portuguese Governments to transfer 50 of the surplus Alpha Jets as part of a military assistance provision in return for the use of facilities at the Portuguese AF base at Beja. Of these 50 aircraft, 5 will be cannibalised to provide spares.

An improved version, referred to as the Alpha Jet 2, with improved avionics and uprated engine is currently being offered for close-air support and weapon firing training.

A total of 510 Alpha Jets serve with 10 air forces around the world. These include Belgium, Cameroon, Egypt, Ivory Coast, Morocco, Nigeria, Qatar and Togo.

FAIRCHILD A-10A

The Fairchild A-10A Thunderbolt II was the first aircraft designed specifically for the close-air support role for the USAF. The first production A-10 took to the air on 10 May 1972.

The A-10 was designed to be highly manoeuvrable at low speeds and to provide an extremely accurate weapons platform. It has a short take-off and landing capability and a useful combat radius. For protection the pilot is surrounded by titanium armour, while the airframe has numerous back-up systems. Fuel tanks are self seal and surrounded by foam, while the main undercarriage is positioned so that the aircraft can land without hydraulic power.

The first A-10s were delivered to the 355th Tactical Training Wing at Davis Monthan AFB in March 1976. A total of six A-10 squadrons were based in the UK from January 1979. From the UK they would deploy to forward operating bases in Germany in times of tension.

A total of 713 A-10As were built for the USAF, of which 26 were later converted to OA-10A for the Forward Air Control role.

During Desert Shield, a total of 144 A-10s were deployed to the Gulf. During Desert Storm the A-10s excelled in the destruction of Iraqi equipment.

The A-10 is fitted with a 30 mm GAU-8/A gun in the nose which can fire 4,200 rounds per minute. In addition, it has eight under-wing hard points plus another three under the fuselage. They can carry up to a total of 16,000 lb of ordnance. This can include iron or Laser Guided Bombs (LGB), Maverick air-to-surface missiles, Sidewinder air-to-air missiles (both illustrated), jamming and chaff/flare pods. In 1993 the last of the 81 TFW, based at RAF Woodbridge were flown out as part of the winding down of US forces worldwide. The only A-10s that now remain in Europe belong to the 81st FS, 52nd FW based at Spangdahlem AB in Germany.

FIAT G-91

The Fiat G-91 was the result of a NATO requirement for a light fighter/strike aircraft that could be a common type throughout the member air forces. The prototype first flew on 9 August 1956.

Due to political reasons the G-91 was only adopted by the Italian and German Air Forces. In 1961 Portugal purchased 40 G-91R4s from Germany following a cancelled order by Greece and Turkey. They saw action in Africa during anti-guerrilla operations in Portuguese Guinea, Mozambique and Angola, although in Angola they were confined to a straightforward reconnaissance role. In 1976 further additions were

made to the Portuguese AF fleet in the form of six G-91T3 two-seat trainers and twenty G-91R3s which were surplus to the German AF.

The last operator of the G-91 was Portugal, which finally retired the last unit in 1993.

This particular G-91 was operated by Esq 301. It is one of a number of NATO squadrons which incorporate the Tiger within their badge. Each year the squadrons get together at a 'Tiger Meet' and often the aircraft are painted with the Tiger.

GENERAL DYNAMICS F-16

The F-16 was the General Dynamics contender for a lightweight
fighter which was intended for the USAF and USN. The contract
for two YF-16 prototypes was placed in 1972 along with another to
Northrop for their YF-17. The F-16 made its first official flight on
2 February 1974, although it had flown unofficially on 20 January
by accident. The USAF finally selected the F-16 in 1975.

In addition to the internally mounted M-61 20 mm cannon, the
F-16 is fitted with nine ordnance stations which can accommodate
a wide range of stores, including bombs, fuel tanks and missiles. It
has a typical range of 852 miles, but this can be extended by in-
flight refuelling. These F-16Cs of 50th TFW are refuelling from a
KC-135R.

GENERAL DYNAMICS F-16A

The bubble canopy was designed to give the pilot unobstructed
forward and upward vision, while over the side and rearward vision
is an improvement on other contemporary fighters. The ejector
seat has a 30° inclination to help the pilot to tolerate the high
G-force encountered. The F-16 is stressed up to 9G with full internal fuel. To help the pilot control the aircraft under such conditions, a side stick replaces the aircraft control column.

GENERAL DYNAMICS F-16
(above, right and opposite)

Production commenced with the single seat F-16A and the F-16B two seat trainer. In January 1979, the 388th TFW at Hill AFB was the first operation unit to receive the F-16. As deliveries progressed, a forward-looking plan was implemented to minimise the costs of retro-fitting new systems in development. As a result all F-16s delivered from November 1980 onwards had built in structural and wiring fitted in addition to a system architecture capable of being expanded to accommodate these new systems quickly and smoothly.

In July 1984 deliveries of the single seat F-16C and two seat F-16D commenced. This new variant had an improved radar with increased range and advanced ECCM. The cockpit was fitted with a wide angle HUD while the HARM anti-radiation missile and new AMRAAM air-to-air missiles, seen here being launched, were added to its inventory. A wide range of improvements to the avionics included the addition of the LANTIRN navigation and attack system, GPS, digital flight controls, automatic terrain following and advanced IFF. In addition to this the airframe has increased take-off and manoeuvring weight limits including a 9G capability and now has an 8,000 hour life.

The use of advanced technology has made the F-16 one of the most manoeuvrable fighters ever built. Airframe weight was reduced through the use of composite materials wherever possible. To reduce purchase and maintenance costs, proven systems were selected from the F-111 and F-15 and integrated into the F-16, giving it extremely effective air-to-air as well as air-to-ground capabilities.

Currently some 3,300 F-16s are operated worldwide, over 2,000 by the USAF. Other operators include Bahrain, Belgium, Denmark, Egypt, Greece, Indonesia, Israel, South Korea, Morocco, Netherlands, Norway, Pakistan, Portugal, Singapore, Turkey (illustrated here on UN patrol off Croatia) and Venezuela. Some of the original F-16As are now being retired, but will probably be refurbished and sold to air forces which are unable to afford new aircraft.

GENERAL DYNAMICS F-16

Large numbers of USAF F-16s were deployed to the Middle East from USA and Europe, including the Air National Guard, during the build-up to Desert Storm. The F-16 was utilised in the ground attack role and proved to be highly capable. The air defence role was undertaken mainly by the F-14s and F-15s, although the F-16s were always fitted with air-to-air missiles for self-defence. When the war ended most of the aircraft returned to their bases.

Some aircraft remained in Saudi Arabia to ensure that the Iraqis did not return to conflict. A UN no-fly zone was imposed on the north and south regions of Iraq. A number of incidents occurred when Iraqi ground units used the ground radar to threaten Allied aircraft, resulting in the Iraqi position being attacked. Occasionally the Iraqi Air Force would probe the no-fly zone. On 27 December 1992, two MiG-25 'Foxbats' were detected within the no-fly zone and F-16s of the 363rd FW were directed to intercept. An F-16D subsequently fired an AMRAAM missile which destroyed one of the MiG-25s – proving the

ability of the aircraft and the new missile.

The deteriorating situation in the former country of Yugoslavia resulted in the declaration of a no-fly zone over Bosnia-Herzegovina. A number of aircraft from different nationalities are involved, including F-16s from the Netherlands, Norwegian and Turkish Air Forces as well as the USAF. These USAF F-16s are on patrol over Croatia. Helicopters of the various warring parties are continually defying the restrictions. These are usually forced to land but take off again once the fighters have cleared. On 28 February 1994 a flight of six Serbian Super Galebs were detected inside Bosnian territory by an E-3. They were warned to land or clear the area but continued with a bombing mission. F-16s of the 526th FS operating out of Aviano were directed to intercept. The first F-16 fired an AIM-120 AMRAAM and two AIM-9M Sidewinders, each of which found a target. The second F-16 fired one missile destroying another aircraft.

GENERAL DYNAMICS F-111

The General Dynamics F-111A was not designed for the fighter role, although it has a fighter designation. It is an all-weather attack aircraft with swept wings, a low landing speed, an economical transit speed and high speed dash. With the wings forward, it is capable of 5,090 km with external fuel tanks.

Deliveries of the first of the 141 F-111As commenced in October 1967. The Royal Australian Air Force took delivery of 24 F-111Cs for the strike role followed by 4 which were modified for tactical reconnaissance. 96 F-111Ds were built with an improved navigation system and air-to-air weapon delivery and served with 27th TFW at Cannon AFB in New Mexico. A total of 94 F-111Es were built, most of which served with the USAFE's 20th TFW at RAF Upper Heyford from 1970. The F-111A was superceded on the production line by the F-111E which had modified air intakes giving an improved engine performance above Mach 2.2. The next variant built was the F-111F for the 48th TFW at RAF Lakenheath. 106 were built with uprated turbofans and the capability of carrying the Pave Tack target designation system. Pave Tack enables the crew to locate, track and designate a target for laser, infra-red or electro-optically guided weapons. The final F-111s built were the FB-111s, which were designed as a two seat, medium range strategic bomber, capable of low level precision bombing in all weathers with the AGM-69A SRAM missiles or nuclear bombs.

Subsequent additional requirements resulted in two conversion programmes. The first was for the defence suppression role. 42 F-111As were fitted with various electronic black boxes including the ALQ-99E – similar to that fitted to the US Navy EA-6 Prowler and re-designated EF-111A Raven. The second conversion programme involved the FB-111As, which were fitted with an improved terrain following radar and conventional weapon release, as well as some new avionics. This aircraft was designated F-111G.

GENERAL DYNAMICS F-111E/F

An F-111F of the 48th TFW, armed with an LGB and AIM-9 Sidewinder. This unit undertook its first combat mission when 18 aircraft were tasked with a bombing mission against Libya. In 1990 about 70 F-111Fs were deployed to Saudi for Desert Storm, while F-111Es were deployed to Turkey and EF-111As flew in support of all the missions.

Later that year, the F-111s were recalled to the USA. Most of the F-111Fs were delivered to 27th FW at Cannon AFB and the EF-111As to 366th OG at Mountain Home AFB. Only some of the F-111Es went to 27th FW, while others went into storage or museums. The last F-111s were withdrawn from the UK in December 1993 after 23 years of service.

GRUMMAN F-14 TOMCAT

The Grumman F-14 Tomcat is the US Navy's two seat carrier borne long range air superiority fighter. It was hoped that the design of the General Dynamics F-111B would meet the requirements of the USAF F-105 replacement and the USN F-4. Despite a major political row, the F-111B programme was cancelled, and the F-14 proceeded. Like the F-111, the F-14 employs the variable geometry wing design giving the aircraft low approach speeds while maintaining a high speed attack capability. Having won the US Navy TFX competition in 1969, Grumman built and flew the first of twelve development aircraft on 21 December 1970.

The roles of the F-14 Tomcat are to provide air superiority for the strike force by clearing a designated airspace of enemy aircraft for out-bound and returning attack aircraft; to provide a Combat Air Patrol (CAP) for the carrier task group; to provide a strike and reconnaissance capability.

The variable geometry wings can be swept from 20° through to 68° enabling the F-14 to fly a slow approach onto a carrier or fly at its maximum speed of Mach 2.34 for an intercept. The angle of the wings can be adjusted manually by the pilot or by the automatic sweep programmer to reduce the workload during a dogfight.

When the wings are swept, a small variable sweep foreplane or glove vanes are used to balance supersonic trim change, and these can be see in action here.

GRUMMAN F-14 TOMCAT

The F-14 Tomcat is capable of carrying a range of weaponry. It is fitted with the AWG-9 radar, capable of identifying and engaging enemy targets at 100 miles range. This is optimised for the long range AIM-54A Phoenix AAM, one of which is being launched in this photograph. This missile is the Tomcat's primary weapon. A General Electric M61A-1 20 mm multi-barrel cannon is fitted in the forward fuselage. A mixed missile combination can range from six Phoenix plus two Sidewinder to four Phoenix, two Sparrow and two Sidewinder.

For the strike role the F-14D Tomcat can carry the AGM-88 HARM anti-radiation missile or a range of bombs up to 6,577 kg. A reconnaissance pod could be fitted, while a later addition is the Tactical Air Reconnaissance Pod System (TARPS) which proved to be highly effective during Desert Storm for battle damage assessment and the monitoring of enemy troop/equipment movements.

In addition to 557 Tomcats delivered to the USN, 80 were delivered to the Imperial Iranian Air Force during the rule of the Shah of Iran. Since he was deposed in favour of the Islamic Republic of Iran and the Tehran hostages incident occurred, the export of spares to Iran halted, resulting in the fleet being reduced to about a quarter of its previous power.
For carrier take-off, the Tomcat is positioned on a steam catapult. The wings are swept fully forward and the nose wheel connected to the catapult ....

GRUMMAN F-14 TOMCAT

Once the Tomcat has been fully prepared for launch, including the raising of a blast defector behind the aircraft, the afterburner is lit and with a thunderous roar it is propelled along the deck by the steam catapult to reach flying speed within a few seconds. On this night take-off the afterburner has been cut once the aircraft has stabilised and then continues off on its task (above). A further F-14 Tomcat and an F/A-18

Hornet are ready for their launch.

The F-14A was initially powered by two Pratt & Whitney TF30-P-412 turbofans producing 20,900 lb static thrust with afterburner. These were replaced in the F-14B/D by the General Electric F110-GE-400 which produces 27,000 lb st. and gives the later Tomcats a greatly improved performance.

HAWKER HUNTER

The Hawker Hunter first flew on 20 July 1951, and went on to become Britain's most successful jet fighter. Over the years a total of 1,985 were built and demand continued after production finished. As a result some 700 were refurbished for re-sale.

The Hunter is armed with four 30 mm Aden cannons in a removable unit for quick re-arming. A range of bombs and rockets as well as external fuel tanks can be fitted under the wings. The Swiss Air Force modified their Hunters to accommodate the Sidewinder AAM.

In addition to the RAF and Royal Navy a total of nineteen different air arms have operated the Hunter, including those of Abu Dhabi, Belgium, Chile (illustrated), India, Iraq, Kenya, Kuwait, Lebanon, Oman, Peru, Qatar, Rhodesia, Singapore, Switzerland and United Emirates.

Although it was a firm favourite with those that flew it, the Hunter is now operated by very few air forces. In early 1994 it was finally withdrawn from the RAF as well as the Omani AF.

ISRAELI AIRCRAFT INDUSTRIES KFIR

The IAI Kfir was built as a result of a French Government embargo of military aircraft to Israel due to the deterioration in Israel's relations with Egypt. As a result the the Israelis decided to build their own version of the Mirage 5 powered by the General Electric J79 engine as a substitute for the French Atar. The complex task of reverse-engineering was undertaken to manufacture the Kfir.

The Kfir C.1 was the initial production variant in the mid '70s. 27 Kfir C.1s were built. This was followed by 185 C2 and TC2 trainers. At the same time a US Marine Corps/US Navy requirement for an aggressor trainer resulted in 25 of the F-21A. Most C2/TC2 were converted to C 7/CT7 in the early '80s and the Nammer will be the next generation.

The Kfir C7 is a Mach 2, multi-role combat aircraft and it can carry a total of 6,085 kg on its seven weapons pylons. These can include a range of bombs, fuel tanks and missiles. It has a useful endurance – typical combat air patrol is 476 nm range with 60 minute loiter when fitted with two Shafrir air-to-air missiles. This can be extended through air-to-air refuelling. It also excels as a low-level, long distance strike aircraft with a high precision attack capability.

The Nammer has been designed as a Mach 2+, long range, multi-role combat aircraft developed from the C7. It is powered by the GE F404-RM12 turbofan engine and this, combined with the delta wing and canard configuration, ensures a superb performance.

LOCKHEED F-104 STARFIGHTER

The Lockheed F-104 Starfighter evolved from early '50s designs which were based on experience gained during the Korean war. At that time speed and altitude were the primary concerns. The prototype Starfighter first took to the air on 7 February 1954.

The Starfighter was conceived at a time when the F-86 Sabre was the fastest USAF aircraft. It was designed to have a maximum speed of Mach 2.2 from the outset, making it a highly ambitious project. The Starfighter resembles a piloted jet engine with stub wings which are only four inches deep at their thickest point.

There were a few problems with the F-104A Starfighter during its early service with the USAF. Despite this, a controversial international order was placed for licensed European production. The F-104G was selected, and production commenced for Belgium, Denmark, Netherlands, Germany and Norway. Further production was undertaken by Canada, Italy and Japan. The order for Germany was the largest with nearly 1,000 Starfighters ordered to fulfil the low-level attack role. This was not an ideal environment for a Mach 2 interceptor. As a result, and also partly as a result of inadequate weather protection and maintenance, the German Air Force and Navy suffered an unacceptably high attrition rate. Subsequent steps to redress the problems resulted in some improvement to the losses, although the poor reputation remained.

In addition to the licence production, Lockheed received orders from Greece (illustrated), Jordan, Pakistan, Taiwan and Turkey.

LOCKHEED F-117

The Lockheed F-117 had been the subject of much speculation for many years. Design and production was undertaken at the Lockheed 'Skunk Works', which has produced other secret types such as the U-2 and SR-71 Blackbird. Although the prototype Lockheed Have Blue prototype was first flown in December 1977, the F-117A remained a mystery until its existence was publicly announced in November 1988 – some five years after it entered service.

Like the F-111, the F-117 has a misleading fighter designation. The actual mission of the F-117A remains classified. However, it is known that this unusual design is actually a precision attack aircraft which employs stealth technology

When some details and photographs were eventually released, the unusual design of the aircraft became apparent. The F-117A was unlike any other aircraft in that none of its surfaces was aerodynamic in the conventional way. The whole aircraft is made up of flat surfaces. This technique, known as faceting, is designed to reflect radar energy away from the transmitters. When combined with Radar Absorbing Material (RAM), the aircraft becomes invisible to any form of radar tracking. The air intakes are covered with a grille to prevent the radar energy being reflected from the inside of the intake or front of the engine. The hot engine exhaust is mixed with cold air and exits through two large slots. This helps to reduce the Infra-Red (IR) signature of the aircraft.

LOCKHEED F-117

The ability of the F-117A to remain invisible to conventional tracking technology means that it does not require a high performance. The F-117 has a typical cruise speed of Mach 0.9. It can carry at least one 2,000 lb bomb in its weapons bay and it is capable of dropping this bomb accurately on the target.

The advantage of the F-117A is that, due to its ability to remain undetected, far fewer aircraft are required to conduct the same objective. During Desert Storm, a standard mission of 32 attack aircraft would require 16 fighter escorts together with 8 Wild Weasel aircraft for radar suppression. In addition, 15 tankers would be required to refuel all of the aircraft. To complete the same mission required only 8 F-117As together with 2 tankers.

A total of 40 F-117As were deployed to Desert Storm, where they were referred to as 'shabba' or ghosts by the Saudis. Although they made up only 2.5% of the USAF combat aircraft, during the first 24 hours, the F-117 was reputed to have struck 31% of the targets. About 1,270 missions were flown against Iraqi targets.

Production of the F-117A was completed after 59 aircraft had been built. A proposal to re-open the production line following the success of the aircraft during Desert Storm and the previous Operation Just Cause in Panama was dropped by Congress.

LOCKHEED/BOEING F-22

The Lockheed/Boeing F-22 was the winner in the competition for the next generation air-superiority fighter referred to as the Advanced Tactical Fighter (ATF). The USAF stated requirement is that the fighter must be capable of penetrating high-threat enemy air space and be able to support Air/Land Battle forces with a first look, first kill capability against multiple targets. The aircraft must be highly manoeuvrable at sub- and supersonic speeds and sustain supersonic speed without afterburner. In addition it must be constructed using low-observable stealth technology. The advanced avionics and weapon systems must be well integrated to enable the aircraft to engage multiple targets successfully.

The 'fly before buy' competition pitched the successful Lockheed F-22 against the Northrop F-23 for the stated requirement for 750

aircraft for the USAF and 546 for the USN to replace the F-14 Tomcat. Already the latter requirement has been reduced to 384. The prototype YF-22 first flew on 29 September 1990.

The US Government's General Accounting Office is trying to delay the deployment of the F-22 by as much as seven years. In an attempt to counteract this, the USAF is warning of the development of the Russian Multi-role Fighter Interceptor. This aircraft, which is also known as the Mikoyan Project 1.42, is considered to have a superior capability to the Su-27 and its improved version – the Su-35. Currently it is believed that the F-15 can match the performance of the Russian aircraft, but it is claimed that the introduction of the MiG before the F-22 might result in a US loss of air superiority.

MCDONNELL-DOUGLAS F-4 PHANTOM

The McDonnell Douglas F-4 Phantom was designed during the early '50s as the private venture XF4H-1 fighter for the US Navy. It first flew on 27 May 1958 and it was soon breaking a large number of performance records, arousing the interest of numerous parties.

The F-4B was the initial production variant for the US Navy. The USAF soon placed an order for 583 F-4s in 1963. F-4C entered service with the USAF as an all-weather tactical fighter. Later production changed to the F-4E which had major system changes to improve its air-to-air and air-to-ground capabilities. The F-4E was optimised as a multi-role fighter with close-air support and interdiction capabilities. It is fitted with a 20 mm Vulcan gun in the nose. The F-4F was specifically built to a German requirement. The F-4G superseded the F-105G in the Wild Weasel role, locating and attacking enemy radar sites. When production of the Phantom terminated, around 5,195 aircraft had been built, of which approximately a quarter were ordered by the intended customer.

The Phantom played a significant role in Vietnam, as well as in the Iran/Iraq wars. More recently, the F-4G successfully participated in Desert Storm.

Sadly the Phantom is now in a decline, having been largely replaced by the F-16 and F-18. An RAF Phantom FG.1 is illustrated below firing its pod mounted Vulcan cannon. All RAF Phantoms have now been retired. However, it still remains a front line aircraft for a large number of countries, including Germany, Greece, Israel and Japan, and many Phantoms have been upgraded.

The last USAF Phantom was withdrawn from Europe in February 1994 as part of the cut-back of US Forces in Europe and the withdrawal of the F-4 from the USAF. Although it has been withdrawn as a fighter, the F-4G Phantom in still operated in the 'Wild Weasel' radar suppression role.

MCDONNELL-DOUGLAS A-4 SKYHAWK

The A-4 Skyhawk is a single-seat lightweight attack/fighter. The Douglas design team had already been investigating a new aircraft in response to a US Navy specification. This proposal greatly exceeded the USN requirement and an order was received for prototypes and pre-production aircraft. The prototype **XA4D-I** took to the air for the first time on 22 June 1954.

The first **A-4A** deliveries commenced during October 1956 to unit **VA-62.** The production progressed with advances in avionics,

weaponry and engine power, to the extent that the A-4 has remained in production for a total of 28 years.

In addition to **US Navy** and **USMC,** variants of the A-4 Skyhawk were sold to Argentina, Australia, Israel, Kuwait, New Zealand (illustrated fitted with Maverick air-to-surface missiles and Sidewinder air-to-air missiles) and Singapore.

The success of the A-4 Skyhawk led to a considerable number of aircraft being re-furbished for re-sale.

MCDONNELL-DOUGLAS F-15 EAGLE

The McDonnell-Douglas F-15 Eagle was designed to be the primary air-superiority fighter for the USAF. It is the first US operational aircraft whose engine thrust exceeds the weight of the aircraft. This, combined with a low wing loading, makes the F-15 highly manoeuvrable with excellent acceleration. The aircraft has an extremely impressive performance. The first flight of the F-15 was on 27 July 1972.

The USAF/McDonnell-Douglas F-15 development contract was a combination of cost-plus-incentives with successive target cost and demonstration milestones. The basic schedule was maintained, despite a few design changes. It is slightly larger and lighter than the F-4 Phantom, whose fighter role it was to replace, but the two Pratt & Whitney F100 turbofans each provided an extra 8,000 lb thrust, nearly 50% additional power.

The F-15 is equipped with an internally mounted 20 mm M61A-1 gun. In addition there are four AIM-7 Sparrow or AMRAAM medium range air-to-air missiles under the fuselage, plus four AIM-9 Sidewinder or ASRAAM short range air-to-air missiles.

The first F-15A was delivered to the USAF in November 1974, followed by the two seat trainer – F-15B – a year later. In June 1979 new versions of the F-15 emerged, which had improved radar and larger internal fuel capacity, as well as the capability to fit conformal fuel tanks. The single seat fighter was designated F-15C and the two seat trainer was the F-15D.

MCDONNELL-DOUGLAS F-15 EAGLE

To maintain a credible defence force, fighters are maintained at an alert status 24 hours a day, 365 days a year. Unidentified returns on ground or airborne early warning radar require investigating, and this results in fighters being scrambled.

Often the offending return is simply the result of the aircraft having a radio or transponder failure. Occasionally, the scramble is for real. In this case the radar return is a Russian Tupolev Tu-95 'Bear' which is flying in international air space to monitor the movements and signals of a NATO exercise. This results in the 'Bear' being shadowed by NATO fighters.

This 'Bear' is being escorted by a USAF F-15C Eagle from 57th FIS from Keflavik in Iceland and an RAF Tornado F.3 from 5 Sqn based at RAF Leeming. Both fighters would normally be fitted with Sidewinder and Sparrow air-to-air missiles, although the F-15 appears to have only two Sparrows.

During the Cold War, this used to be a regular occurrence However, following the improvement in East/West relations, this has become a rare event.

USAF F-15s were deployed to the Gulf during Desert Storm to reinforce those flown by the Royal Saudi Air Force, to protect Saudi airspace and to provide fighter cover for Allied strike aircraft. As a result the F-15s saw a great deal of action, especially in the early days of the war, when Iraqi fighters were scrambled to meet Allied aircraft. It did not take long before the the Iraqis realised that they were completely outclassed.

The Iraqi Air Force fighter force included the highly capable MiG-29 or Mirage F.1, but the Allied strikes were damaging many of the ground-based radar and control centres. This left the fighters to rely on their own radar to track and attack hostile incoming aircraft. By turning on their radar, they gave away their own position, and usually ended up being shot down by one of Allied fighters. This particular F-15 has two Iraqi kills painted below the cockpit.

MCDONNELL-DOUGLAS F/A-18 HORNET

The McDonnell-Douglas F/A-18 Hornet was the result of a competition for a lightweight fighter for the USAF and US Navy. The submission of the F-17 by Northrop was in competition with the General Dynamics F-16. In the end the F-16 was selected for the USAF, while the F-17 was developed and built by McDonnell-Douglas into the F/A-18 Hornet for the US Navy, which had stated a requirement for 1,350 aircraft. The first F/A-18 took to the air on 18 November 1978.

The Hornet entered service with the US Navy in 1982. As a fighter it could carry Sidewinder and Sparrow air-to-air missiles. The wing tips fold upwards to reduce the footprint of the aircraft. Even on US Navy carriers space is at a premium, and the Hornet's ability to fold the wing tips helps to ease the problem. The F/A-18 is fitted with the APG-65 multi-mode radar which enables it to track up to ten targets simultaneously .

The F/A-18C and the two seat F/A-18D appeared in 1987. These were fitted with a much improved computer system, improved EW and ejector seat, the IR Maverick ground attack missile and the capability of operating the new AMRAAM missile.

The Hornet has been given a night-attack capability by the inclusion of a Forward Looking Infra Red (FLIR) system and a Thermal Imaging Navigation Set (TINS). This resulted in the designation F/A-18D, while a further variant – the RF-18D – is a two seat reconnaissance aircraft, fitted with electro-optical and IR sensors plus a pod mounted sideways looking radar.

This formation of F/A-18Ds of VMFA(AW)-553 of the USMC is participating in the UN monitoring of the air exclusion zone over Bosnia.

Following the success of the Phantom, the Hornet was designed with a multi-role capability. The change of role simply entailed a change of weapon fit, fitting or removal of attack sensors and changing the avionics mode. Hence the unique designation of F/A (Fighter/Attack).

The flexibility of the F/A-18 was demonstrated on a mission during Desert Storm when a flight of 4 F/A-18s from VF-81 were tasked to attack an Iraqi airfield, armed with three 2,000 lb bombs plus a pair of Sparrows and Sidewinders. 35 miles from the target, and with the air-to-ground selector set, they were warned of 'Bandits' by a Hawkeye AEW aircraft. The pilots re-selected for air-to-air mode and acquired the MiG-21s. One pilot fired two missiles and another a single missile. Both MiG-21s were destroyed. The pilots re-selected their attack mode and completed the mission as briefed. As a result a MiG-21 'kill' was painted on the nose.

MCDONNELL-DOUGLAS F/A-18 HORNET

Above is one of the 875 F/A-18 USN and USMC Hornets being launched from USS America, while below is another example on dawn patrol off Croatia. They are flown by some 40 tactical squadrons which are based on 12 aircraft carriers and at 25 air stations. The US Navy considers the Hornet as a cornerstone of its air power and plans to continue buying the Hornet through to 2015.

Over 1,200 F/A-18 Hornets have been delivered to the United States Navy and Marine Corps as well as to the Air Forces of Canada, Australia, Spain and Kuwait. In addition orders have been received from Finland, Malaysia and Switzerland.

THE MiG FAMILY

A unique formation of MiGs of the Indian Air Force. Led by a 102 Squadron MiG-25, the formation comprises a MiG-21M of 101 Squadron nearest, next to a MiG-23MF of 224 Squadron. On the far side is a MiG-29 from 223 Squadron next to a MiG-27M of 9 Squadron.

The Indian Air Force continues to maintain a modern air force due to the periodic tension along its borders with Pakistan and China. This tension occasionally breaks out into conflict. As a neutral country, India obtains weaponry from sources in both the East and the West, but is also working hard to establish its own production capabilities, in order to reduce this dependence on other countries. Hindustan has built Jaguars and various MiGs either from kits or

manufactured completely.

Many recent orders for aircraft from various countries are of a similar nature, with local participation dependent on the local capabilities. Some countries construct some of the parts, while others specify final assembly from manufactured kits. In the more industrialised countries with larger orders, assistance with establishing full production may be the deciding factor in which aircraft is finally ordered. In today's world the sale of military aircraft, or any hardware for that matter, is far more competitive and the customers are in a strong position to make their demands.

MIKOYAN GUREVICH MiG-21 'FISHBED'

The Mikoyan MiG-21 'Fishbed' became the main Soviet fighter following its entry into service in 1959. The design of the lightweight fighter ran in parallel with the Su-7 and Su-9. Initially it was designated Ye-5 and first flew on 16 June 1955. In addition to limited avionics, it had a limited fuel capacity, which diminished its endurance.

The MiG-21PF 'Fishbed-D' was the first effective member of the MiG-21 family. It was fitted with a pair of the newly developed K-13 (AA-2 'Atoll') IR air-to-air missiles, but the cannon had to be deleted to reduce weight. It had an increased fuel capacity and a new radar. It proved to be the basis of a range of sub-variants.

The next major sub-type was the MiG-21PFMA 'Fishbed-D' with increased fuel capacity, as well as provision for under-wing and under-fuselage fuel tanks. It could also carry an under-fuselage gun pod, and a variety of weapons could be carried on the under-wing pylons, including rocket pods and air-to-air missiles. These missiles now included the radar-homing 'Advanced Atoll'.

The MiG-21bis 'Fishbed-N' represented a further sub-type which had a re-designed lighter airframe with further increased fuel capacity, as well as modern avionics.

The Indian Air Force ordered a number of the MiG-21 family variants, of which most were built under licence by Hindustan. These Indian Air Force MiG-21FLs are operated by 8 Squadron. Further exports were made to China, with subsequent production by Shenyang as the F-7.

MIKOYAN GUREVICH MiG-21 (above)

When production was completed, it was estimated that some 12,000 MiG-21s had been built over nearly 30 years. Operators have included Afghanistan, Algeria, Bangladesh, Bulgaria, Czechoslovakia, Egypt, Finland, East Germany, Hungary (illustrated), Indonesia, Iraq, North Korea, Poland, Romania, Syria, North Vietnam and Yugoslavia.

MIKOYAN MiG-23 'FLOGGER' (below)

The Mikoyan MiG-23 'Flogger' is a medium weight fighter that was designed in the early '60s. It was first seen in prototype form at the 1967 Aviation Day fly-past at Domodedovo. The MiG-23 is armed with a 23 mm GSh-23 cannon and can be fitted with four AA-8 'Aphid' plus two AA-7 'Apex' air-to-air missiles. Later variants can also operate the AA-11 'Archer'.

In addition to the members of the CIS (Commonwealth of Independent States) the MiG-23 has been operated by Afghanistan, Algeria, Angola, Bulgaria, Cuba, Czechoslovakia (illustrated), Egypt, Ethiopia, the former East Germany, Hungary, India, Iraq, North Korea, Libya, Poland, Romania, Syria, Vietnam and Yemen.

MIKOYAN MiG-25 'FOXBAT'
(above)

The Mikoyan MiG-25 'Foxbat' was designed to combat the threat posed by the Mach 3 B-70 bomber planned for the USAF. Although this was subsequently cancelled, the MiG-25 development continued, and the reconnaissance proto-type flew on 6 March 1964 and the fighter proto-type on 9 September 1964.

Capable of Mach 2.8, the MiG-25 utilised steel rather than titanium to try to reduce the pro-tracted development period. As it was, the MiG-25 did not enter service with the Soviet Air Force until 1970.

The MiG-25 is armed with four AA-9 'Amos' air-to-air missiles.

Some 300 MiG-25s have been built and are flown by the air forces of Algeria, CIS, India (MiG-25R of 102 Squadron illustrated), Iraq, Libya and Syria.

MIKOYAN MiG-27 'FLOGGER-D'

The Mikoyan MiG-27 'Flogger-D' is a ground attack variant of the MiG-23. It is fitted with five weapon pylons, onto which a range of bombs, rockets and missiles (up to 4,000 kg) can be carried. It has an internally mounted multi-barrel cannon under the belly. The nose has been redesigned to include avionics, and later models have a laser range finder instead of the intercept radar.

It is operated by the CIS tactical air forces and Naval Aviation. In addition Hindustan licence builds the MiG-27M for the Indian Air Force.

MIKOYAN MiG-29 'FULCRUM' (above)

The Mikoyan MiG-29 'Fulcrum' is the Soviet answer to the Western type of fighter capabilities. It is a break away from the traditional Soviet types, such as the lighter MiG-17/19 and MiG-21, which were limited in their range, and the heavy-weight MiG-25, which had high speed capability at the expense of manoeuvrability. The MiG-29 is powered by a pair of the fuel efficient Isotov RD-33 low bypass ratio turbofans. The first prototype flew on 6 October 1977.

These colourful Mig-29s are painted in the air combat colours of 28 and 47 Squadrons, Indian Air Force.

The MiG-29 has retractable doors on the air intakes to prevent debris being sucked from the ground into the engines. While the nose wheel is on the ground and the engine running, these doors shut and a number of small doors on the top surface of the wing open to allow air to be drawn into the engine.

MIKOYAN MiG-29 'FULCRUM'

The radar has a range of 100 km and is of a pulse-doppler type with a look down/shoot capability. It has a large IR search/track receiver mounted in a dome in front of the cockpit. It is armed with a 30 mm cannon and can carry a range of air-to-air missiles, including the AA-10 'Alamo' and AA-11 'Archer' on six pylons plus an external fuel tank under the fuselage.

The MiG-29 is powered by two Klimov/Sarkisov RD-33 turbofans, which develop 11,110 lb st. dry and 18,300 lb st. with re-heat.

The MiG-29 is replacing the MiG-21, MiG-23, Su-15 and Su-17. It is currently operated by CIS, Cuba, Germany, India, Iran, Iraq, North Korea, Poland, Romania, Slovakia, Syria and Yugoslavia.

MIKOYAN MiG-31 'FOXHOUND'

The Mikoyan MiG-31 is a two seat, all-weather fighter which has been optimised for high- and low-level operation. It is a development of the MiG-25, and first flew on 16 December 1975. It can track ten targets simultaneously and mount a simultaneous attack on four of them. The Mig-31 is armed with a 23 mm cannon together with four R-33 (AA-9 'AMOS') long range radar guided missiles, two R-60 (AA-8) 'Aphid' medium range IR guided missiles and four short range missiles. The MiG-31 is capable of 3,000 km/hour and has a range of 720 km, although this can be increased to 1,400 km by reducing speed to Mach 0.85 and fitting under-wing fuel tanks.

MITSUBISHI F-1

The Mitsubishi F-1 is the fighter variant of the T-2 trainer. Very similar in appearance to the SEPECAT Jaguar, the Mitsubishi T-2 trainer was first flown on 20 July 1971. The F-1 is a multi-role fighter with the rear cockpit space used to accommodate the additional avionics and the canopy faired over. A T-2 was modified into the F-1 prototype and first flew on 7 July 1975.

A total of 77 Mitsubishi F-1s were built to replace the F-86 Sabres of the Japanese Air Self Defence Force which had become obsolete. It is powered by the Rolls Royce Adour 102, a lower powered version of the same engine in the Jaguar. The F-1 can carry a range of bombs, rockets, fuel tanks and missiles on its four under-wing and single under-fuselage pylons in addition to a single 20 mm M61 cannon.

Eventually it is intended to replace the F-1 with the Mitsubishi FS-X – a Japanese modified and built F-16.

MITSUBISHI FS-X

The Mitsubishi FS-X is a single seat fighter developed from the General Dynamics F-16 for the JASDF. It is planned to replace the Mitsubishi F-1 with the FS-X from late 1987 as well as with the Phantom. The intention is to build 130 aircraft, but this could well be increased up to 200.

NANCHANG A-5 'FANTAN'

The Nanchang A-5 first flew on 4 June 1965.

The A-5 is a single seat, twin engined, supersonic attack aircraft developed from the F-6, which in turn was derived from the MiG-19. The re-design of the MiG led to a large increase in fuel capacity. The A-5's primary mission is to provide close-air support for ground forces. For this role the A-5 was fitted with additional hard points under the wings. It is capable of carrying a range of bombs or rockets, as well as guns on its six underwing and four fuselage hard points. It is

also fitted with a pair of 37 mm NR-30 cannons in the wing-root. For the fighter role, the A-5 is fitted with PL-7 or Sidewinder air-to-air missiles and gun pods.

The 'Fantan' entered service with the Chinese Air Force and Navy in the late '70s. The Pakistani Air Force was the first export customer, eventually ordering 52. Other customers include Bangladesh and North Korea. Nearly 1,000 A-5s have been built.

NORTHROP F-5A FREEDOM FIGHTER (above)

The Northrop F-5A/B was the successful bidder for the US require-ment for a lightweight fighter to be supplied under Military Assistance Programme (MAP). It was first flown as the private ven-ture N-156C on 30 July 1959, and the first production F-5 took to the air in October 1963.

The F-5A and two seat F-5B were named Freedom Fighter, and were armed with 2 nose mounted 20 mm M-39 Browning guns. In addition a wide range of under-wing stores can be fitted onto the four hard-points plus another under the fuselage. Wingtip launchers make it possible to carry a pair of Sidewinder missiles.

Eventually over 1,040 F-5A/Bs were built with additional produc-tion by Canadair, CASA and Fokker. They were operated by Canada, Ethiopia, Greece, Iran, Libya, Morocco, Netherlands, Norway, Philippines, Republic of China, South Korea, Spain, Thailand, Turkey and Vietnam.

NORTHROP F-5E TIGER II (below)

The Northrop F-5E Tiger II was a private venture version of the F-5A. It first flew in March 1969 with General Electric J85-GE-21 turbojets which gave an additional 23% more power. A number of modifications were made to improve the manoeuvrability.

By the time production of the F-5E and two seat F-5F was complete, a further 1,400 aircraft had been built. The USAF and US Navy bought a number for aggressor training, and the aircraft also served with nine-teen other countries.

The F-5 continues to be of interest, as there are a number of re-fur-bishment programmes to update the aircraft which will ensure that the F-5 will be flying many years from now.

PANAVIA TORNADO GR.1

The Panavia Tornado commenced as a six-Government feasibility study for a future all-weather strike aircraft in 1968. Construction of nine prototypes was undertaken, resulting in the first flight of P01 on 14 August 1974.

The Tornado is a variable-geometry, all-weather NATO combat aircraft. It was designed and built by a tri-national company – Panavia – which comprises British Aerospace (42.5%), MBB (42.5%) and Alenia, which was previously Aeritalia, (15%). A production line was established with each company. BAe built the front and rear fuselages, MBB the centre fuselage and Alenia the wings. Final assembly of each aircraft was conducted in each country.

A Memorandum of Understanding was signed for a total of 809 aircraft in two variants – 640 IDS and 165 ADV – plus four of the pre-series to be brought up to IDS standard. The first to be built was the

IDS (InterDictor Strike) version, which was for the air forces of UK, Germany and Italy plus the German Navy. This was followed by the ADV (Air Defence Variant) which was developed specifically to meet a Royal Air Force requirement. Initial production was designated the F.2 and later production, the F.3.

Subsequently two other variants of the IDS have been built. The first for the RAF was for reconnaissance and designated GR.1A. The second was to meet a German requirement for an anti-radar 'Wild Weasel' and this was designated ECR (Electronic Combat and Reconnaissance).

The RAF Tornado GR.1 is commencing a mid-life upgrade which will result in the GR.4 variant and the Italian Air Force has commenced the modification of sixteen of their IDS for the ECR role.

PANAVIA TORNADO F.3

During the Gulf War, Tornados were deployed from the UK and Italy and, together with those of the Royal Saudi Air Force, some 3,250 sorties were flown against Iraqi targets. Since then eight RAF Tornado F.3s have been based in Italy and fly in support of United Nations to enforce the 'No Fly Zone' as part of the Operation 'Deny Flight' (the NATO operation to prevent aircraft from flying in Bosnia-Herzegovina).

The RAF ordered 165 of the ADV to replace the Lightnings and Phantoms in the interceptor role. Initial deliveries were the Tornado F.2 variant, which were soon replaced by the Tornado F.3.

The recent diminishment of the threat from the Eastern Block has resulted in a surplus of Tornado F.3s. Italy has entered into an agreement to lease 24 as a stop-gap between the ageing Starfighters and the delivery of the Eurofighter 2000.

A fully armed RAF Tornado F.3 intercepts a Soviet Air Force Tupolev Tu-95 'Bear' over the North Sea (above). During the Cold War this was a regular occurrence. However, now that there has been an improvement in relations with the East, these probing flights have become a rarity.

PANAVIA TORNADO F.3

The Tornado F.3 has an excellent loiter capability with its economical Turbo-Union RB.199 turbo-fan engines and with wings swept forward. It can fly Combat Air Patrol (CAP) for over two hours 555–740 km from its base and include ten minutes of air combat. In 1987 a Tornado F.3 made the first un-refuelled crossing of the Atlantic by a British fighter in which it covered 4,077 km in 4 hours 45 minutes. This impressive range for a fighter can be increased by air-to-air refuelling.

All of the Tornado variants can carry air-to-air missiles, the IDS and ECR for self protection and the Tornado F.3 or ADV for its primary role. An adapter can be fitted to the inboard wing pylons of the Tornado IDS and GR.1, so that the Sidewinder air-to-air missile can be fitted. This enables this strike variant of the Tornado to carry the missile on all missions without losing any of the pylon stations. The German Tornado can also be fitted with the HARM anti-radiation missile for radar suppression.

PZL-130 TURBO-ORLIK

The Polish Turbo-Orlik is a tandem seat basic and advanced turbo-prop trainer. Developed from the re-engined piston powered Orlik, this new variant took to the air for the first time on 13 July 1986.

Although designed as a trainer, the Turbo-Orlik has been constructed with three hard-points under each wing. While limited to a total of 800 kg of under-wing stores, the Strela IR air-to-air missiles can be carried in addition to external fuel tanks, small bombs, rockets or gun pods.

A total of 48 PZL-130TBs have been ordered for the Polish Air Force, and this and subsequent variants of the Turbo-Orlik are being promoted to and evaluated by various other countries.

ROCKWELL/DASA X-31A

The Rockwell/DASA X-31A EFM is an Enhanced Fighter Manoeuvrability aircraft being developed jointly by the US and Germany. MBB (now part of **DASA**) commenced work on a project in 1977 and was joined by Rockwell in 1983. A feasibility study was made in 1984, and in 1986 the funding was provided for two prototypes to be built. The first X-31A made its maiden flight on 11 October 1990.

The purpose of this single seat research aircraft is as a

demonstrator for expanding the flight manoeuvering envelope. Following the fitting of thrust vectoring paddles to the rear nozzle, the thrust from the engines can be deflected by some 10°. This together with the foreplanes, wing and tail control surfaces enables the X-31A to remain controllable and it is an effective fighter at slow speeds and high angles of attack.

SAAB 105

The **SAAB 105** is a twin seat multi-purpose aircraft designed for training and light ground attack purposes. The aircraft was designed as a private venture and first took to the air on 29 June 1963.

The first order for 130 of the **SAAB 105** was placed by the Swedish Air Force in 1964, and these aircraft were designated Sk.60. In addition to training and light attack, the **SAAB 105** has been used for communications, for which the two ejector seats are removed and four fixed seats fitted. Other roles include reconnaissance

and target towing.

The **SAAB 105OE** was ordered by the Austrian Air Force in the late '60s and tasked with the air defence and ground attack role. With limited fighter capabilities, the Austrian Air Force is having some of its SAAB 105s modified to carry the Sidewinder AAM. This is due to the need to maintain the integrity of its airspace following incursions by aircraft of the warring parties in the former state of Yugoslavia

SAAB J-35 DRAKEN

The SAAB J-35 Draken was designed as a single seat bomber intercep-tor in the late '40s. It has a unique double delta wing shape. Powered by a single Rolls Royce Avon jet engine, the Draken was intended to be just supersonic. The prototype first took to the air on 25 October 1955.

The Draken entered service with the Swedish Air Force in March 1960. Two months prior to this the aircraft reached Mach 2 – a feat which the shorter range English Electric Lightning took two Avon engines to match. The Draken is fitted with nine hard-points, three under each wing plus three under the fuselage. These are capable of

carrying a range of stores, including Sidewinder or Falcon (illustrated) air-to-air missiles and external fuel tanks, in addition to its internally mounted 30 mm Aden cannon.

Other roles for the Draken have included ground attack, for which 1,000 lb bombs can be carried, and reconnaissance. For the latter role a pod was developed initially, but later the cameras were mounted in the nose.

About 550 Draken have been built for the Swedish Air Force, with additional production going to Austria, Denmark and Finland.

SAAB J-37 VIGGEN

The SAAB J-37 Viggen is the highly capable product of the neutral Swedish arms industry. The Viggen was designed at the outset to be a multi-role combat aircraft to replace the Lansen and Draken in most of their roles. The Viggen is an integrated part of the Swedish STRIL 60 air-defence network. The first Viggen prototype took to the air on 8 February 1967. The AJ-37 was the first production Viggen variant and replaced the Lansen in the ground attack role with the fighter/interceptor role as secondary. The SH-37 replaced the Lansen in the sea surveillance role followed by the SF-37 as the overland reconnaissance variant replacing the Draken. Both variants can carry

air-to-air missiles for self defence. The SK-37 two seat trainer is also based on the AJ-37 Viggen.

The JA-37 Viggen is the single seat interceptor variant and has numerous differences to the AJ-37. The Volvo RM8A has been replaced by the RM8B, giving a much improved performance. The Ericsson PS-46 pulse-doppler radar is fitted, with the result that two JA-37 Viggens on coastal patrol can now monitor as much airspace as a squadron of Drakens. The JA-37 Viggen is fitted with a long range 30 mm Oerlikon cannon, while Sidewinder and Sky Flash air-to-air missiles are carried on pylons.

SAAB JAS-39 GRIPEN

The JAS-39 Gripen is the latest aircraft from the Swedish manufacturer SAAB. Design of this single seat fighter, attack and reconnaissance aircraft commenced in 1980 with a go-ahead given in 1983. The maiden flight of the prototype Gripen was made on 9 December 1988.

The Swedish Air Force has a requirement for 340–350 aircraft to replace the remaining Drakens, as well as the AJ-37, SH-37, SF-37 and then the JA-37 Viggens eventually.

The Gripen is armed with an internally mounted 27 mm Mauser cannon with a range of air-to-air missiles on the pair of hard-points under each wing and one under the fuselage. In addition a rail enables a missile to be fitted to each wing-tip. Missiles that can be carried include Sidewinder, Sky Flash and AMRAAM, while air-to-surface missiles include the Maverick or RB-15F anti-shipping missile.

SEPECAT JAGUAR

The SEPECAT Jaguar was developed jointly by Breguet in France and BAC in the UK. It was originally designed as a light tactical attack and training aircraft. This was to meet a common aircraft requirement for the French Air Force and the RAF. The first prototype took to the air on 8 September 1968.

The Jaguar E (Ecole or School) two seat trainer was the first to enter service with the French Air Force, which ordered 40. The first entered service in May 1972. The 160 Jaguar A (Appui or Attack) deliveries followed.

The Jaguar single seat and two seat trainer have identical weapons carrying capabilities. They are fitted with one under-fuselage hard-point plus a pair under each wing. They are capable of carrying an external load of up to 4,535 kg. A pair of internally mounted 30 mm DEFA 553 cannons are fitted. A wide range of stores can be carried, including bombs and rockets, as well as missiles including the Armée de l'Air AN.52 tactical nuclear bomb, Belouga cluster bombs and Durandal runway cratering missile. The trainer is capable of undertaking operational missions if required.

A French Navy prototype was built, but the project was cancelled in 1973.

SEPECAT JAGUAR GR.1

The RAF Jaguar is basically similar to its French Air Force counterpart, but is fitted out with an advanced inertial navigation system and weapon-aiming system.

A total of 165 plus 35 T.2 two seat trainers were built for the RAF with a further 3 trainers for the research establishments.

In recent years the Jaguar has been extremely busy. In 1991 No 6 (Composite) Squadron was deployed to the Gulf and flew numerous bombing and recce missions in support of Operation Desert Storm. When that halted, the Jaguars were re-deployed to Incirlik in Turkey to provide air cover for the Kurds of Northern Iraq against the Iraqi military which was attacking them. During this period the Jaguars were painted pink.

Eventually the Jaguars were replaced at Incirlik by Harrier GR.7s. However, the Jaguars were re-painted grey and redeployed to Italy, to fly missions over Bosnia-Herzegovina to police the UN imposed No-Fly Zone.

The French were not interested in promoting the Jaguar for overseas orders, as it would compete with potential Mirage sales. BAC made the effort, and this resulted in sales to Ecuador, Nigeria and Oman, while India took some aircraft and kits for assembly prior to the opening of its own production line.

The RAF Jaguars were fitted with the Sidewinder air-to-air missiles on over-wing pylons prior to being deployed for the Gulf War. Up until then the Jaguar carried no self defence weapon other than a pair of internally mounted 30 mm Aden cannons. During Operation Desert Storm the RAF Jaguars carried a range of bombs and rockets on their under-wing pylons.

SEPECAT JAGUAR GR.1

The RAF currently operates three squadrons of Jaguars. Two, Nos 6 and 54 Squadrons, are tasked with the ground attack role, while the third, No 41 Squadron, is for tactical reconnaissance. A fourth unit, No 16 (Reserve) Squadron, provides the operational conversion. All of these units operate a combination of the Jaguar GR.1A and T.2A. They are all capable of flying the same operational missions. The only difference between a ground attack and a reconnaissance Jaguar is a centre-line pod, which contains a range of cameras.

Since the Jaguar was modified for the operational deployment to the Gulf, aircrews now have an extra element added to their training syllabus – the missile practice camp which culminates in the firing of a Sidewinder missile.

SHENYANG F-6

The Shenyang F-6 is a Chinese built MiG-19. The MiG-19 entered service with the Soviet air defence force in the mid '50s and was phased out of production around 1960. Prior to the breakdown in relations between Moscow and Peking, the Russians had supplied the Chinese with some MiG-19s. When they were unable to get any more aircraft or spares for the ones that they had, the Chinese commenced reverse engineering the aircraft.

The first F-6 flew in 1961 and entered production shortly afterwards to become the Chinese Air Force standard fighter. It is estimated that as many as 1,500 were built before production ceased.

Exports were made to a number of countries, including Albania, Bangladesh, Egypt, Ethiopia, North Korea, Pakistan (illustrated), Somalia, Tanzania, Vietnam and Zambia.

SHENYANG F-7

The Shenyang F-7 is a Chinese built MiG-21. As with the F-6, the F-7 was the result of reverse engineering the Soviet aircraft. It first flew in 1964, but the performance was so poor that the F-6 was to remain in production until 1979.

Eventually problems with the F-7 were resolved. Fitted with an improved WP-7BN engine, an extra 30 mm cannon and a number of other modifications, the F-7M Airguard boasted an effective Mach 2 performance.

Further improvements resulted in an aircraft with sales potential, and the F-7P Skyguard was exported to Pakistan.

The FT-7 (illustrated) is the two seat trainer variant of the F-7. For the role of fighter, the F-7M is normally fitted with air-to-air missiles plus 30 mm cannon, although it is capable of carrying 500 kg bombs or rockets in the ground support role. For weapon training the FT-7 can be fitted with a 23 mm gun pod plus a range of weapons on the five hard-points, including the PL-2A air-to-air missile.

In addition to the Chinese Air Force, the F-7 operators include Albania and Pakistan.

PL-2A AIR-TO-AIR MISSILE
The CATIC PL-2A is a Chinese built AIM-9 Sidewinder air-to-air missile look-alike. This is an Infra-Red (IR) guided air-to-air missile that can be fitted to almost any fighter aircraft.

SHENYANG F-8 II 'FINBACK-B'

The Shenyang F-8 II 'Finback-B' is a single seat twin engined supersonic air superiority fighter. It has a secondary capability of ground attack. The development of the F-8 commenced in 1964 and the first prototype flew on 5 July 1969.

Production of the original F-8 was limited, although some 100 F-8 Is were built. These were superseded on the production line by the F-8 II, which was built in small batches. There was a proposal to upgrade the F-8 II with Western avionics under the US government Peace Pearl programme. Following the events of Tiananmen Square, the US Government embargoed any deliveries of avionics in 1989. As a result, China is attempting to produce the upgrade domestically.

The F-8 is armed with an internally mounted 23 mm Type 23 twin-barrel cannon. It is fitted with seven hard-points, including one under fuselage. These can carry a range of weapons including PL-2B and PL-7 air-to-air missiles, air-to-ground and air-to-air unguided rockets, bombs and external fuel tanks.

SOKO J-22 ORAO/AVIOANE IAR-93

The Soko J-22 Orao/Avioane IAR-93 is a joint Yugoslav/Romanian design for a single seat close support, ground attack and tactical reconnaissance aircraft. It has a secondary role as an interceptor. The joint project commenced in 1970 to fulfil the common requirements of both air forces. Each company made a pair of single seat prototypes with a simultaneous maiden flight on 31 October 1974. These were followed by construction of a two seat trainer by each company.

Development then continued with 15 pre-production aircraft by each company. Production of 26 IAR-93A single seat and 10 two seat aircraft commenced, followed by 165 IAR-93Bs. In the meantime production of 15 of the Yugoslav IJ-22 single seat and INJ-22 two seat aircraft commenced, followed by 165 J-22s.

The power plant for these aircraft is based on the Rolls Royce Viper 632 non-afterburning turbojet or Viper 633 with afterburner.

All members of the J-22 Orao/IAR-93 family are fitted with two 23 mm GSh-23L twin barrelled cannon, bombs, rockets, while the IAR-93B can carry up to eight air-to-air missiles.

SOKO G-4 SUPER GALEB

The Soko G-4 Super Galeb is a two seat basic/advanced trainer and ground attack aircraft. The programme was launched in 1973 as a replacement for the Soko G-2 Galeb and the Lockheed T-33. Construction of the prototype commenced and it made its maiden flight on 17 July 1978.

The Super Galeb can be fitted with a 23 mm GSh-23L twin barrel rapid fire cannon in a ventral gun pod. Up to six under-wing hard-points can be used to fit a range of bombs and rockets up to a total of 1,280 kg. In addition wing tip rails enable a pair of AA-8 'Aphid' air-to-air missiles to be carried.

Construction of three prototypes, including a ground test airframe, was followed by six pre-production aircraft. Production commenced to meet a Yugoslavian Air Force requirement for 150 aircraft. However, the future of these is now uncertain following the break-up of Yugoslavia. A total of twenty have been delivered to the Myanmar (Burmese) Air Force.

SUKHOI SU-22 'FITTER-K'

The Sukhoi Su-22 'Fitter-K' is a single seat variable geometry ground attack fighter and reconnaissance aircraft. The design was developed from the Su-7 with the outer wing section pivoted. A prototype Su-7 was constructed and made its first flight on 2 August 1966. It was first publicly displayed at the Domidedovo Aviation Day Display in July 1967.

The Su-22 is the export variant of the Su-17. It is fitted with eight stores pylons, onto which a range of air-to-surface missiles, rockets and bombs, including nuclear weapons, can be fitted. This is in addition to the pair of 30 mm NR-30 guns. This Polish Air Force Su-22M4 'Fitter-K' is fitted with a pair of AA-8 'Aphid' air-to-air missiles and four H-25MP anti-radiation ground-to-air missiles.

SUKHOI SU-22 FITTER (above)

The Su-17 led to the Su-20 and Su-22 variants, which were widely exported. Apart from some 1,000-plus Su-17s, which were delivered to the Soviet Air Force – now the CIS Air Force – many other countries ordered the Su-20/22. These included Afghanistan, Algeria, Angola, Czechoslovakia (illustrated), East Germany, Egypt, Hungary, Iraq, North Korea, Libya, Peru, Poland, Syria, Vietnam and Yemen.

SUKHOI SU-24 'FENCER' (below)

The Sukhoi Su-24 'Fencer' is a two seat variable geometry bomber, reconnaissance and EW aircraft. Development commenced in June 1964, and the prototype first took to the air in June 1967.

The Su-24 first became operational in 1976. It can be armed with nuclear weapons, TV or laser guided bombs, or air-to-surface missiles such as AS-7 'Kerry', AS-10 'Karen' and AS-12 'Kegler'. It can also carry bombs and rockets, as well as R-60 AA-8 'Aphid' air-to-air missiles.

Over 900 Su-24s were delivered to the Soviet Air Force and Navy, with further deliveries to Iraq (although most are now in Iran), Libya and Syria.

SUKHOI SU-25 'FROGFOOT'

The Sukhoi Su-25 'Frogfoot' was designed for battlefield close support and is the Russian equivalent of the Fairchild A-10. Development of this aircraft commenced in 1968 and the prototype took to the air on 22 February 1975.

Production commenced in 1978 and the first squadron was deployed to Afghanistan for co-ordinated close support with Mil-24 gunships.

The Su-25 is armed with a 30 mm twin barrel gun and has ten under-wing weapons pylons, on which it can carry a wide range of bombs, rocket pods, fuel tanks and gun pods up to 4,400 kg. It is also fitted with a laser rangefinder/designator for the accurate delivery of LGBs. Two small outboard pylons can be used to carry R-3S AA-2D 'Atoll' or R-60 AA-8 'Aphid' air-to-air missiles.

A number of variants of the Su-25 family exist. These include the Su-25K, which is an export version of the Su-25. Su-25UB is a two seat operational conversion/weapons trainer, with the Su-25UBK being the export version. The Su-25UT (also designated Su-28) is similar to the Su-25UB but without a weapons carrying capability. The Su-25UTG is a navalised variant which has been fitted with an arrester hook. Su-25BM is used for target towing. The Su-25T is the improved Su-25, while the Su-25TK is its two sea trainer variant.

The Su-25 is operated by the CIS Navy and Air Force, Afghanistan, Bulgaria, Czechoslovakia, Hungary and Iraq.

This specially painted Czech Air Force Su-25 is appropriately marked for its tank busting activities.

SUKHOI SU-27 'FLANKER'

The Sukhoi Su-27 'Flanker' was designed as an air superiority fighter and first flew in prototype form on 20 May 1977.

The Su-27 is similar in shape to the MiG-29, but is larger than the F-15, with which it has a comparable performance. A stripped and lightened Su-27 was fitted with slightly more powerful engines in 1986, in an attempt to break some of the contemporary records.

It is powered by two Lyulka AL-31F turbofans which give the Su-27 a thrust to weight ratio of approximately 1:1 – similar to the F-15. This engine is extremely rugged in performance, as has been frequently demonstrated in the West by aerial maneouvres, such as the tail slide or the Cobra, where the aircraft, flying at slow speed, is pitched up into the vertical before returning back to normal flight attitude. A mesh screen is deployed across the engine intakes when the aircraft is on the ground and the engine is running to provide protection from FOD.

The Su-27 is fitted with a 30 mm GSh-301 cannon for close range attack but is designed for beyond visual range interception and is ususally fitted with AA-8 'Aphid', AA-10 'Alamo' or AA-11 'Archer' air-to-air missiles.

VOUGHT F-8E (FN) CRUSADER

The Vought F-8E (FN) Crusader first flew on 25 March 1955 as a US Navy air superiority fighter. Later examples were flown by the USMC but have now been withdrawn from service.

The Philippines bought 25 ex-USN F-8Hs plus a further 10 airframes for spares. These were withdrawn in 1988 due to economy and serviceability.

The only other operator of the Crusader is the French Navy, which ordered 42 F-8E(FN)s, of which the first flew on 11 April 1964. They have been used to equip two squadrons of the French Navy.

The Crusader features a wing that pivots 7° to increase the angle of attack yet maintain the pilot's vision during low speed flight. The Crusaders for the French Navy were also fitted with extra lift enhancers to enable them to operate successfully from the smaller carriers – the Clemenceau and the Foch. The Crusaders can be armed with either the Sidewinder or Matra Magic (illustrated) air-to-air missiles on rails either side of the fuselage. In addition the F-8 has four integrally mounted 20 mm Colt-Browning cannons in the nose.

The French Navy plans to keep the last remaining F-8E(FN)s flying until they are replaced by the Rafale M in 1998.

YAKOVLEV YAK-38 'FORGER'

The Yakovlev Yak-38 'Forger' is a V/STOL multi-role fighter designed for use by the Soviet Navy using the experience gained from the Yak-36. It first flew in 1971 and deliveries began in 1975.

It is fitted with one vectored thrust Mikulin/Soyuz R29V-300 turbojet with one pair of nozzles aft of the wings. In addition it has two vertically mounted Rybinsk RD-36-35FVRs, which are utilised for the V/STOL landing and take-off sequences only.

The Yak-38 has four weapons pylons, onto which a range of bombs, gun pods and missiles can be fitted, such as the air-to-air AA-8 'Aphid' or AS-7 'Kerry' for the air-to-surface role.

Approximately 75 Yak-38s are thought to have been built and were deployed aboard the Kiev Class of aircraft carriers, but currently their future is uncertain.

YAKOVLEV YAK-141 'FREESTYLE'

The Yakovlev Yak-141 'Freestyle' is a single seat carrier-based V/STOL fighter/attack aircraft. Although the project for this aircraft commenced in 1975, it was 1991 before any details became available. The prototype of the Yak-141 first flew in March 1989.

The Yak-141 is planned to replace the Yak-38 aboard the Kiev Class carriers. It is powered by a Soyuz R-79 turbofan, and a door beneath the nozzle enables it to be vectored 65° down for short take-off and 95° downward and forward for vertical landing. Two vertically mounted Rybinsk RD-41 liftjets are located immediately aft of the cockpit.

The Yak-141 lodged a number of claims for international records to the FAI including time to height with a payload in the STOL category.

INDEX